SAVING MUNIC

Lesley Yarranton is a former journalist, television researcher and translator. She was one of the first western journalists to live in and report from East Berlin after the Fall of the Berlin Wall. She has since worked in Paris and Washington DC. She lives in the Cotswolds with her family.

Saving Munich 1945

The story of Rupprecht Gerngross

Lesley Yarranton

REVISED EDITION

THE REAL PRESS

www.therealpress.co.uk

First published in 2020 by the Real Press. New edition, 2021.   www.therealpress.co.uk   © Lesley Yarranton

ISBN (print) 9781912119783
ISBN (ebooks) 9781912119776

In memory of
Mike Harskin

Chapters

Our aim was to "show the world that there was a Germany other than the Nazi one... and, by doing so, show that German people could prove, through deeds, how truly vile they found National Socialism..."

("dem Ausland zu zeigen, daß es noch ein anderes Deutschland gibt, als das nationalsozialistische und gleichzeitig dazutun, daß hier deutsche Männer ihre Ablehnung dem Nationalsozialismus gegenüber durch die Tat beweisen wollten. ***Freiheitsaktion Bayern 1945 by Dr Rupprecht Gerngross und Dr Otto Heinrich Leiling circa 15.6.45 (BayHStA/Abteilung IV, Handschriftensammlung 2347)***

Foreword

It is nearly thirty years since I first heard of a small group of German army officers rising up against Hitler to save Munich in the dying days of the Nazi regime.

I was a foreign correspondent, who had moved to Berlin within days of the Wall being torn down, and had been tracking the rise of neo-Nazi groups starting to flourish in covert, underground cells across the forlorn expanses of the defunct, communist German Democratic Republic.

Most were bunches of disenfranchised, shorn-headed youths, brought together by a lethal cocktail of nostalgia for the glories of Germany's past and hostility to what they saw as greedy western corporations rushing to profit from cheap land, a cheap workforce and the undamming of a large market of hungry consumers.

One group, led by a former member of the German Freedom Movement *(Die Deutsche Freiheits-bewegung),* was beginning to emerge as an umbrella organisation for multiple underground neo-Nazi splinter movements.

It stood out with its sophisticated *modus operandi*: slick corporate e-mails and "business headquarters" in an affluent suburb of Munich.

It did not take too much digging to gain access to Bela Ewald Althans: he was to be found at a meeting promoting the work of David Irving, the controversial right-wing British historian at the centre of the Goebbels' diaries row (Irving had been banned from Germany for "reasons of state security" and Althans was acting as his agent, smuggling him in and out of the country to give talks to spread the word about how the Holocaust was nothing but a 'great lie').

Saying he feared the possibility of a bomb attack at his office, Althans insisted on conducting the interview at his apartment. It was an interview I will never forget. Perched on the edge of a chair in a modest flat in an ordinary Munich street, I listened as Althans, an imposing six foot figure, dressed head-to-toe in black, talked darkly about his plans for the movement.

We sat for over an hour, surrounded by framed photographs of Hitler and Nazi memorabilia while, in a corner of the dimly-lit room, black and white footage from Third Reich movie-maker Leni Riefenstahl's fawning productions flickered silently on a loop.

He talked calmly and confidently but grew agitated when I asked him about his decision to base his movement in Munich, rather than in the new capital of Berlin. Was it influenced by the loyalty Munich had historically shown to Hitler?

Yes, he said, it was the city that had proudly supported the Führer but – at the end – "even in this loyal city" Hitler had been betrayed. One young captain had "shamelessly" turned his own soldiers and led military units against the regime in the last days of the war in a bid to force an early surrender. The timing, he argued, was the worst humiliation.

The *coup* staged by the young captain was brief – the American forces entered the city just days later - but it was a story I had never heard before. The Stauffenberg 'Valkyrie' plot to assassinate Hitler with a bomb was well-known. This was very different. The idea of younger, lesser-ranking rebels challenging the Führer at his deluded end was fascinating. What happened to them?

I hastily scribbled a note in the margin of my notebook but my searches for reports of the young captain the next day drew a blank and I began to doubt the accuracy of what I had been told. A news editor's summons sent me back to Berlin and I dismissed them from my thoughts.

But nearly thirty years later, upon reading historian David Boyle's revelations of the furious struggle in and around the BBC over wartime broadcasting and its controversial sacking of the man in charge of European news, a figure sprang out of its pages like a ghost from the past.

Noel Newsome, the BBC's director of European broadcasts, had heard of a group of German soldiers turning against the Nazis, seizing the state broadcasting station to launch a general uprising and fighting the SS on the streets. The young captain's broadcasts had been recorded and reported on by the BBC.

Newsome had interviewed Captain Rupprecht Gerngross. He had helped to save the city of Munich and many of the lives of the 400,000 people still living there.

He filed an in-depth account to the *Times* newspaper only for it never to appear. It had been pulled from the presses at the last moment after a newspaper executive sent it to the Foreign Office to be 'vetted for policy'. It was rejected on the grounds that it was "not thought desirable to suggest that there were 'good Germans'". As a result, Newsome's account, written in 1945, could not be read until 2018, when his autobiography was finally published.

The reason why my efforts to find information about Gerngross and his men all those years ago had proved so difficult, soon became clear. Their story had lain untold because it served as a reminder of painful, war-end humiliations, highlighted people's own failure to act and, for the most part, wasn't believed.

It took research from material released to archives following the death of Gerngross in 1996 – and Newsome's account – for a more forgiving evaluation of the rebellion to quietly emerge from decades of suppression. It has led to, what some would argue, is the long, overdue erection or restoration of monuments in small towns and villages across Bavaria commemorating the German soldiers, who tore the Nazi regalia from their uniforms and died fighting Nazis.

This, finally, is their story.....

Rupprecht Gerngross in front of a microphone, date unknown.

Introduction

A raucous chorus from the barracks hall below interrupts the officer's thoughts. Downstairs, the men of his company are jostling together, sharing jokes and swigging fiery *Obstler* schnapps to keep out the winter chill. He has opened the small window of his room, needing the cool, fresh air, but now returns impatiently to the typed notes of his speech.

The knock comes, as arranged, at 22.00 hours precisely. A young sergeant puts his head around the door. "Company ready, Sir."

The speech-writer, a tall, handsome young Wehrmacht captain, half-smiles back. Downstairs, the men are preparing to drink a toast beneath a portrait of Hitler that hangs over the fireplace. Just as they did at the same hour last Friday evening – the Führer's 56th birthday.

But tonight the toast is to themselves - a small band of underground resistance fighters sworn to rid Germany of Nazism. Their immediate aim is to make sure that Hitler's current orders to destroy Munich and starve out its people rather than have it fall into enemy hands, will not be fulfilled.

Barracks commander Rupprecht Gerngross leaves

his room, heads downstairs and surveys his motley group of men. Through the haze of smoke and alcohol fumes he can see the tension in their faces. His breath feels short, his throat tight, but when he starts speaking, his voice is 'calm and sure'.

"The moment has come," he begins, "to free ourselves from the Nazi yoke.... and end the senseless fighting and the laying waste of our country." Anyone, he tells his men, can back out now if they choose. "But whoever follows me now must stick it out to the end." He is discharging them, he says, from the obligations of the 'Hitler oath' – the compulsory pledge of personal allegiance every Wehrmacht soldier must make to the Führer.

"Hitler has broken *his* oath to you many times over," he explains. "You are no longer bound to honour him with 'obedience unto death." He pauses, facing them square-on. "Last month, we received an order - a devastating one for the morale of our troops. It says that we must, on sight, shoot dead anyone retreating or 'breaching the faith' in the way we are all doing here tonight. So if any one of you wants to shoot me dead where I stand – do so now."[1]

A moment's silence, then a cheer goes up. No one, even though they have yet to hear details of exactly what is expected of them, wants to pull out. Even the handful of tame 'old Nazis', kept among their numbers to ward off the suspicions of the barrack spies, is caught up in the enthusiasm.

Strips of torn, white sheets are brought in, along with piles of weapons as Gerngross rattles through the instructions. Within hours, all over the city, groups of armed men wearing white armbands from the Freedom Action of Bavaria *(Freiheitsaktion Bayern: FAB)* are on the move, ready to take up position.

These men are not hardened fighters laden with medals and illustrious battlefield records, but a troop of humble, military translators: ordinary middle-ranking officers with little more than bicycles and a few tanks at their disposal. Yet they understand strategy, and how to best use what little they have. Working from the grassroots up, they have tapped into a vein of patriotism and loyalty and are about to stage an extraordinary act of resistance under the very noses of the Gestapo.

They believe that public disillusionment, stoked by years of hardship, repression and military failure could now, at last, break the grip of National Socialism; that their uprising, carried on a broad, popular tide of citizens' support, can overturn a Nazi regime intent, whatever the cost, of fighting to the bitter end.

First they are going to seize, kidnap or kill three top Nazis who hold the immediate key to political and military power in the southern corner of the Reich. By destroying telephone exchanges they will impose an information blackout, preventing news of their insurrection from reaching Hitler's bunker in Berlin and delaying the *Waffen SS*, Hitler's fanatical shock troops, from launching counter-measures.

They will then lead an armed uprising of the people against bedrock Nazi loyalists, halt a 'death march' of

Jews from concentration camps and surrender the shreds of Hitler's once-mighty Reich to the approaching Allied forces.

They aim to replace the Führer's dictatorship with a return to a civilian, democratic government and the rule of law. They will use the seized radio stations and newspapers to let people know what they are doing, urge them to help them overthrow the Nazis and call on Hitler's soldiers to lay down their arms.

This no insurrectionist fantasy, but a plan, framed long ago in the dimly remembered days before Hitler's rise to power twelve years earlier. That they have been able to develop it in secrecy in a police state, covertly enlisting the support of several military units, astonishes even themselves.

Wriggling through the small cracks in the tyranny's armour, they have established contacts with other resistance groups: the Kreisau Circle led by Bavarian-born Count Claus von Stauffenberg, leader of the 'Valkyrie' plot to assassinate Hitler with a briefcase bomb, the spiritual

White Rose students, whose anti-war leaflets called for active opposition to the Nazi regime; even a monarchist group known as the Sperr circle, which seeks to supplant Hitler by restoring Bavaria to a monarchy under an exiled Crown Prince.

So far, all such attempts at resistance have ended in failure and a date with the executioner, achieving little beyond the further tightening of Hitler's grip. With each feat of survival, the Führer is able to embellish the narrative of his invincibility as the 'chosen' one – the embodiment of the ancient myths of Aryan superiority. It seems that the more plots there were, the more deep-rooted the delusion of *Führerliebe* (adoration of the Führer) grows.

The Munich conspirators, however, will play the game differently. Patiently. They have been thinking about this since early June, 1944 when the first D-Day landing craft came ashore at Normandy. Back then, they realised, there would be too great a risk and too little support. A second plan to move once the Americans crossed the Rhine, the great natural moat around Germany's heartlands, also had to be abandoned. Gerngross and his resistance fighters have calculated they will only have enough military support to hold their city for around six hours. They cannot put their plan into action until the US Army is a "safe day's march" away.

Gerngross now knows that this moment has arrived and within hours of his speech, *The Freiheitsaktion Bayern's* trucks are rolling out of the barrack gates. It is just before midnight on April 27 1945. Twenty four hours later, Hitler will lead Eva Braun, pale-faced and sleepless, from their apartment in the Berlin Führerbunker to its map room, where guests are waiting to witness their macabre marriage. Two days later, Eva will take poison and, as Russian shells rain down on the bunker, the 56-year-old Führer will shoot himself in the mouth. [2]

But the war will not end with a joint suicide in a bunker. No one outside Hitler's close inner circle will know for days that the Führer is dead, and the powerful pistons of the Nazi war machine are firing almost as strongly as they did back in the glory days of 1933. The terror apparatus of a Reich built to last a thousand years remains intact, and a population fed on propaganda continues to believe the Nazi message of inevitable victory.

As Allied bombers drone over the city pounding it to rubble and adding to the massive food shortage and refugee crisis, clerks in Munich's ministry buildings continue to fill in forms in order, their rubber stamps slamming down with force and fierce sense of purpose.

Less than 48 hours will pass between Gerngross sending his men into action and the Americans breaking through the last enemy lines surrounding the city, but in those crucial hours Hitler's final telegrammed instruction to 'proceed at once and mercilessly' against all traitors is to be ruthlessly obeyed and as the Nazi regime, in the unbridled violence of its death throes, rears up against its attackers, thousands more have yet to lose their lives.

But, for now, all that matters to Gerngross and his men is bringing an end to the "senseless loss of life" and protecting their families and their homes. They are determined that, if no one else will save Munich, *they* will.

Richard and Helene Gerngross in Shanghai in 1925 (top) and preparing to leave Shanghai for Germany in March 1926 with their three children: Barbara, Rupprecht (centre) and his brother Richard Otto.

Rupprecht Gerngross, aged 9, in 1925, appearing in a play based on a Chinese fairy tale. He spoke of his childhood in Shanghai as "a happy one.... We grew up with an open-minded attitude to the world." Pictures courtesy of the photo library of Studienwerk deutsches Leben in Ostasien (German Life in East Asia Foundation) reg. nos. P0434, P6838 and P0438.

1

Ambition, idealism and imagination lay at the heart of life in the Gerngross family. Rupprecht Gerngross' father, Richard, born in the picturesque ski town of Garmisch Partenkirchen within sight of Germany's highest mountain, the *Zugspitze*, was proud of his Bavarian and Swabian heritage and had a reverence for tradition and outdoor life.

He studied medicine, qualified as a doctor and opened a small hospital in a suburb of Munich. As a young boy, he had been fascinated by tales of the Far East and the China seas, and when restlessness struck in his early thirties, he made up his mind to see the world for real. Specialising in the treatment of tropical diseases, he became a ship's doctor.

Aboard a transatlantic steamer, operated by the Hamburg American (Hapag) Line, he was captivated by a young German passenger. Helene, a teacher, was on her way to study in the USA. Romance blossomed, but Helene, was set on fulfilling her dream of teaching English in America.

They parted, but her kindness and open-mindedness had made a lasting impression on

Richard, while she could not forgot the ship's doctor with his rugged good looks. They stayed in touch and, seven years after their first meeting were married.

By now, Richard's travels had taken him all over the Far East, but it was Shanghai, the great Chinese trading city on the Whangpoo that had won him over, and he hoped his new bride would be equally smitten. She was, and they stayed for over a decade, among a rich wave of families from Europe, including many fleeing Tsarist anti-semitism and revolutionary upheaval in Russia, building new lives under the Shanghai International Settlement.

Despite their immersion in the rich cultural life of city that was making a name for itself as 'The Paris of the East', the couple kept Germany close to their hearts and, when their two sons and daughter were born, they turned the back garden of their elegant Shanghai home into a patch of the rural Fatherland they had left behind.

Hedges and bushes that could withstand the Asian climate were pulled up from the gardens of Bavarian relatives, shipped over and transplanted; the small bare patch of land was soon awash with flowers and shading greenery that evoked the vines and chestnut trees that hung over the beer gardens back home.

By the time the couple's youngest son was born in 1915, hens, rabbits, goats, dogs and a donkey could be found wandering around outside the Gerngross' back door – much to the consternation of the neighbours. Thus the young Rupprecht, possibly gaining early instruction in how to 'compartmentalise' areas of his life, grew up thinking it nothing unusual to be living in the heart of Shanghai with a miniature Bavarian farmyard outside the back door.

While Rupprecht's father, a tall, confident man, cut a startling figure striding along trails in the Chinese mountains in his traditional *Lederhosen* and Tyrolean-style hat, his wife would follow behind, leading her children, singing Alpine hiking songs or reciting poems.

"My father, having been raised by a long line of Bavarian forest wardens, chemists and master brewers always felt Bavarian," he once said[1] But the couple had an equally deep-rooted desire for their children to enjoy a "liberal and cosmopolitan" upbringing in a port where trade and the Shanghai International Settlement drew people from all over the world.

They appear to have been an exceptional couple. Richard Gerngross' exuberant but deeply-held Catholic beliefs being matched in equal measure by his wife's quieter, sterner Protestant convictions. These arose from a strict upbringing in Hamburg (to the horror of her husband-to-be, her father appeared scandalised at the suggestion that they 'go dancing').[2]

She nevertheless accepted her parents' religious strictures and after leaving school attended a teaching college founded by the seventeenth century Lutheran preacher August Francke, with the aim of sending teachers out into the world to do 'good works'.[3]

It cannot have been easy to reconcile such religious differences but Rupprecht believed his parents led by example, displaying the tolerance they expected of their children. They also instilled a deep love of languages and their role in understanding the minds of others. German was spoken at home, both parents mastered Chinese, the maid spoke only French, while English was the official language of British-controlled Shanghai.

It was the ease with which he learnt to slip between languages, cultures and attitudes in an international community – "growing up in *"Weltoffenheit"* (literally, an openness to the world) – that informed many of Rupprecht's decisions in later life. [4]

Professor Richard Gerngross found work at the port's newly-founded German Medical School, which the German government had plans to expand, and which would later house the city's prestigious Tongji University, still renowned today for its medicine school.

Rupprecht attended Shanghai's Kaiser-Wilhelm School for the children of German families; at home his mother ensured his rigorous instruction in German art, music and literature.

After-school riding classes meant he developed impressive equestrian skills, laying a foundation for what his parents believed would be a future military career.

Many years later, he recalled with fondness experiencing "the greatest harmony" living as a small child at home with his family; his father constantly busy with patients, nevertheless always managing to find time for his young family. [5]

But these idyllic days were coming to an end. In

late 1926, the first rumblings of what would become civil war spread across China with armed confrontations between the forces of the Nationalist government and Communist Party militias.

The conflict was sending a troubling message to the large community of European and American families who had made their homes in enclaves like Shanghai. For Richard and Helene a return to Germany began to look like a safer option.

Back home, the new, post-World War I Weimar Republic had been formed, with a democratically-elected government headed by Paul von Hindenburg. New treaties were signed with old enemies, and Germany was allowed to take a seat at the League of Nations. Stability and progress were the optimistic watchwords of the new order, and to the Gerngross family, anxiously following developments in China, a promising signal that it was time to return home.

Pretty Oberhaching, ten miles south of Munich, made a deep initial impression on the 11-year-old Rupprecht, whose knowledge of Germany came almost entirely from books and his parents' stories. Above its medieval streets loomed a 17th century mansion, *Schloss Laufzorn*, built by a Bavarian duke, a pilgrim's church with foundations dating back to the eighth century *Heilig-Kreuz (Kreuzpullach)* and, many years later, he fondly recalled the vanilla-soaked aroma of freshly baked cakes and strong coffee from the streets lined with traditional *Konditoreien*.

After the inevitable culture shock – neighbours were horrified to find him dressed in thin cotton shirts in the middle of winter – Rupprecht quickly adapted to his new life in Germany, and enjoyed discovering his extended family.

His parents revived old friendships and became a familiar sight on the dance floor of Munich's elegant Regina Palast in Maximilian Strasse, an old haunt from their courtship days.

Professor Gerngross found work in the nearby town of *Bad Wiessee* on a lakeside in the beautiful Bavarian Alps. A newly-opened spa resort, it attracted a wide range of patients keen to undergo hydrotherapy treatment in the waters of its natural sulphur spring.

At school, Rupprecht threw himself into his studies, and appears to have adapted well to life in his 'new' country. But no sooner had the family settled in than political storm clouds began to gather over Germany, as the Weimar government floundered in the face of economic crisis and growing social disorder. Munich's newspapers contained frequent accounts of the rise of a radical new movement – the National Socialist German Workers' Party, led by Adolf Hitler.

Even at school, Rupprecht noticed the changes. "There were individuals there, a few National Socialists," he wrote, "who felt good and were delighted to be able to wear a brown shirt, and often they would surreptitiously put a black tie with it and call themselves *'Jungvolk'* ('German Youngsters', the name given to boys aged 8–14 in the Hitler Youth)."

He felt more at home with activities organised by the local scouts, where he found the leaders were patriotic "but never tried to influence you in this or that direction". [6]

Soon, signs of imminent disaster were everywhere. Burdened by massive reparation payments imposed after the war, Germany was sinking into bankruptcy. As interest rates soared, and the value of the nation's currency sank, the Gerngross family, like millions of others faced a struggle to survive. Richard and Helene had planned to renovate their modest, semi-detached house in *Deisenhofen*, but paying the builders became harder by the day.

Rupprecht recalled seeing his father's humiliation, as he arrived home bent double under the weight of the rucksack he was forced to use to carry their wages – only to find the money had devalued so much during the short journey it was: "barely enough (for them) to buy a bread roll". [7]

By 1929, the fourteen-year-old Rupprecht was seeing political agitators working the queue of jobless men stretching from Munich's unemployment office in *Maistraße* almost three-quarters of a mile to the *Sendlinger Tor* archway. Pitched battles were breaking out between left and right-wing organisations with proxy private armies called *Freikorps,* largely made up of the angry and the jobless.

Centuries of conservative Catholicism had given Munich a spectacular skyline of church spires – the very name *München* means, literally, 'of monks' – but now a new kind of religion, one based around the cultish veneration of one man and his message was taking over the streets.

As Alan Bullock writes in his book *Hitler: A Study in Tyranny*: "Few towns in the Reich were as sensitive to the mood of unrest as Munich: its political atmosphere was unstable and exaggerated towards one extreme or the other." [8]

There were many who would never forget the short-lived six months of 'people's rule' in Bavaria when, during the civil unrest of 1918 Bavaria was freed from eight centuries of reign by the Wittelsbach royal family. Now agitators, with dark intent, were once again finding it to be a rich feeding ground.

Bullock cites the famous reply given by Munich's Chief of Police, Ernst Pöhner, when asked if he knew there were political murder gangs in Bavaria: 'Yes, but not enough of them.'[9] At his side stood his assistant, a quiet, little-known *Oberamtmann* (city councilman) called Wilhelm Frick, a lawyer by profession, whose wily skills in obtaining permission for political rallies and demonstrations were already in use by Hitler and who was soon to reap his reward: the privileged post of Reich Minister of the Interior.

In the year the Gerngross family returned to Germany, a failed Cologne bank clerk with a deformed right foot called Joseph Goebbels had begun to appear alongside Hitler at National Socialist beer hall rallies in Munich and had been offered the position of Gauleiter (district leader) of Berlin.

He had always nurtured ambitions to be a writer and his skill with a narrative soon became evident. Striking new posters with loud slogans in red ink began to appear on the streets of Munich. The world was divided into the nation's saviours and those who would destroy it. A string of beer-hall battles and brawls propelling the right-wing extremists into news headlines on an almost daily basis bore the master propagandist-to-be's imprint.

It is quite likely that some of the patients Professor Richard Gerngross was treating were NSDAP officials; one of the earliest Nazi flags to be hoisted was seen on the southern shore of the Tegernsee Lake in 1920 on a pier close to the church at Rottach and several high-ranking Nazis were known to have homes there.[10]

Among their new neighbours in *Oberhaching* was the only woman to have taken part in the 1923 Beer Hall Putsch, the notorious 'Sister Pia' (Eleonore Baur). A former midwife, who reputedly met Hitler on a tram, she would become one of the first to use manual labour from a local prisoner camp *(München-Schwabing)*. Groups of prisoners were "reportedly whipped and ordered to do manual labour" including "cleaning her house, tending her garden and even building children's toys for her". [11]

It hardly seems possible that such activities could escape unnoticed in their small community but if Richard Gerngross feared for the future, he hid those concerns from his children, and hoped for a peaceful resolution.

Confirmation that there was unlikely to be one came with a town meeting at *Oberhaching's Hotel Weißbräu* in the Spring of 1932. It was called to debate the likely re-election of the 84-year-old

President von Hindenburg. Rupprecht attended with his parents.

Hindenburg's seven-year term of office was expiring and Hitler, whose Nazis were now the second largest party in the Reichstag, was pushing hard for a greater role in government. Win or lose, Hitler seemed certain to play a much greater role in Germany's future.

The *Weißbräu* meeting began as the usual, low-key, convivial turn-out of townsfolk mixing political discussion with good-natured banter over foaming Steins of beer. Easter came early that year and the hotel, which played a central part in the life of the town, was gaily decorated with bunting and painted eggs. It was the kind of traditional Bavarian gathering Richard and Helene had missed while pursuing their lives abroad and they had set off from home with their youngest son with little idea that it was to change the course of their lives.

Rupprecht, who was 16, does not recall all the details of the meeting – only its ominous end. As it was about to conclude, with a customary rendition of the national anthem, the *Deutschlandlied*, a uniformed Nazi Party *SA-Sturmbannführer* (Major) stepped on to the stage and took charge of proceedings.

On his tunic was one of the most prestigious decorations bestowed by the Nazi party – the *Blutorden*, or 'Blood Orders' signifying that he had fought alongside Hitler in the 1923 putsch and was one of the earliest members to serve the party.

Tonight, he announced, the Horst-Wessel Song, dedicated to a bogus Nazi martyr, would replace the *Deutschlandlied* and at this, several of his followers began singing. [12]

There was no disguising Richard Gerngross' fury. The Nazis' use of cherished and respected German titles and symbols to give a veneer of respectability to what he viewed as their dishonest political motives had long rankled with the doctor. Rupprecht wrote later of how deeply offensive his father had found the Nazis' trying to subvert national symbols for their cause.

Professor Gerngross stormed out of the meeting, dragging Rupprecht after him. The boy had never seen his mild-mannered father so enraged and would not forget the night of his first exposure to the fanatical face of Nazism.

From that moment, life in the Gerngross household changed dramatically. Richard and Helene formed the nucleus of a small resistance group of members seeking ways of working covertly against the Nazis without putting their families, homes and livelihoods at risk. For in January 1933, Hindenburg, the old Prussian warhorse, had caved in, given Hitler the Chancellorship, and within a month the Nazis were in total control of Germany.

At first the Gerngrosses and their friends would meet in the comfortable drawing room of Richard and Helene's home, disguising the gatherings as 'social evenings'. Later, for added security, they moved to a shed in their back garden. As soon as he had finished his homework, Rupprecht would attend schooling of a different kind. In the dim light of the hut among piles of garden tools, he would listen to family friends plotting ways of fighting a regime that, in every corner of German life, was now showing its tyrannous teeth.

The meetings "included people from as far away as Nuremberg and included all shades of political opinion – conservative through to communist."[13] Uniting them was a belief that that however tough the odds, however hard the fight, the Nazis had to be opposed.

Among this circle were businessmen, lawyers, and most usefully, a senior journalist, who taught Rupprecht how to "read between the lines" of the Nazi *Völkischen Beobachter* newspaper. "He showed us how to distinguish between truth, lies and concealment in what was served up as news," wrote Rupprecht later.

These secret gatherings did not last long before careless talk brought stormtroopers to the front door. One afternoon in 1934, the Gerngrosses returned home to find every room in their house ransacked, along with the attic and the shed. Doors had been wrenched from hinges, cupboards and drawers emptied, their contents left shredded and scattered around the rooms.

There followed a visit from the local NSDAP official, who, in the course of an outwardly civilised meeting, made no attempt to conceal a threat to ruin the family financially. "He told my father: 'You must join the National Socialist party, Herr Professor. If you do not, we will denounce you as a Jew". There was no known Jewish blood in the family, but the effect this would have on his livelihood barely needed stating.

Picking up the nearest object that came to hand, his father calmly replied: 'Mein Herr, if you do not leave, I will throw you out.' The official turned and left. [14]

But the incident marked the family out forever more as suspect. The meeting in the Gerngross parlour may have been short but the Nazi apparatus had a long memory and *twelve* years later, a harsh vengeance was extracted. When a British bombing raid damaged several houses in the street, teams of Hitler Youth workers appeared, with orders to make repairs.

The Gerngross house was left untouched. "They wouldn't give us a single roof tile," remembered Gerngross, " let alone help us... my father was a marked man." [15]

By the time the young Rupprecht had taken his A Levels in 1934, he had grown into a "large, heavy-set young man". He was also "scholarly, cultured and good-natured – a most unlikely combination for a revolutionist," American historian John Toland noted in his book, *The Last 100 Days: The Tumultuous and Controversial Story of the Final Days of World War II in Europe.* [16]

Yet he was no leftist radical. The first organisation he joined was the *Stahlhelm*, the junior branch of the conservative nationalist German ex-servicemen's organisation, the 'Steel Helmet League of Front

Soldiers', named after the coal-scuttle shaped helmets worn in the First World War. Fiercely patriotic, the group's main demand was the scrapping of the Treaty of Versailles – the source of the punitive war reparations that most Germans believed were crippling their country.

Young Gerngross had been impressed by accounts of the group protecting farmers against marauding Communist gangs. He respected the distance they kept from the Nazis and, like his father, thought they represented one of the few hopes of a route out of political chaos and a return to the "order of the old Reich".

He soon found himself under the guidance of a leader he could genuinely respect. Colonel Adolf Seitz, head of the Bavarian Steel Helmets, maintained a deep faith in moral principles, which he advocated as a guiding light out of the darkness.

Seitz was a friend of Carl Goerdeler, himself an active opponent of Hitler who would eventually be hanged for his part in the 1944 'Valkyrie' conspiracy. He saw a clear distinction between honest patriotism and the bloodthirsty, fanatical nationalism of the Nazis. It was possible, he taught his young adherent, to put your own country first without resorting to the hatred and denigration of others.

The young Rupprecht took these lessons to heart, describing his mentor as: "an inspiration," and: "a man, who, while driven by the urgent need to prevent the National Socialists coming to power, was nonetheless prepared to serve in the army out of a sense of national, patriotic duty." He noted: "It was the quiet, faint expression of a dream, then, that the Reichswehr would be in a position to stem the tide." [17]

Hitler, though, was mistrustful of the Steel Helmets and within a year of seizing power in 1933, merged them with the paramilitary *Sturmabteilung* (SA: Storm Division), whose primary role was to provide protection for Nazi rallies and who had played a significant role in his personal rise to power.

The horror with which this creeping para-militarisation was viewed by the regular army soon filtered back to the young recruits in the Steel Helmets. Shaped by traditions of discipline and honour dating back to Frederick the Great, the army viewed the *Sturmabteilung* (SA) as no more than an undisciplined mob of brawling street thugs.

Seizing every opportunity he could to boost NSDAP membership, Hitler ordered all Stahlhelm members to be automatically enrolled in the party. By May 1937, Rupprecht, his brother and father had all been issued with membership cards.[18] The young Gerngross, now 20, was in any case ready to start his university studies but needed to meet the requirement of a spell of volunteer work before he could be accepted.

Encouraged by Colonel Seitz's teachings that there were still many "decent men" in the Reichswehr, who could be trusted to do the right thing, he would volunteer in one of the German army's specialised mountain units: the 19th infantry regiment Bavarian Alpine Mine Launcher Company. The two men said goodbye, but it would not be long before their paths crossed again.

Colonel Adolf Seitz. Gerngross, who served under him as a 16-year-old in the youth wing of the Bavarian 'Steel Helmets' described him as a 'role-model'.Seitz was a friend of Carl Goerdeler, who was hanged for his part in the Valkyrie conspiracy.

2

Gerngross left the Bavarian Alpine regiment after a year, with a report that he showed military promise, but the cogs of the Nazi machine were beginning to turn.

In March 1935, the year he began his law studies at Munich University, Germany announced it would re-arm and introduce conscription to preserve 'peace for herself and the rest of Europe'. Goebbel's voice shook with suppressed emotion when he read the proclamation to foreign correspondents. [1]

A few months later, SS Reichsführer Heinrich Himmler founded the *Lebensborn* Project (literally: "Fount of Life"), a 'fast-breeding programme' to boost numbers of Aryan children. Medals were awarded to women who bore the most, while the babies of unmarried women were seized and given to 'racially pure' foster parents, particularly those of the SS.

Day-by-day, the tentacles of the National Socialist German Workers' Party (NSDAP) were winding themselves around almost every aspect of daily German life.

The columns of the so-called 'Honour Temples' containing the sarcophagi of the sixteen early Nazis who died in Hitler's failed Beer Hall putsch of 1923 had risen over Munich's *Königsplatz*, not far from the university's lecture halls, their eternal flames lighting the square at night. Passers-by were expected to hail the plaque bearing the names of the 'martyrs' with a Nazi salute.

One of Gerngross' contemporaries recalls his father's shock at being ordered to remove his hat when a troop of Nazi supporters marched past him in the street parading the Blood Flag – stained with the martyrs' blood – one of the NSDAP's most revered possessions. [2]

Rupprecht had seen enough. "I sought the chance to leave the Reich borders as quickly as I could," he said, and soon transferred part of his law and governance studies to the London School of Economics.[3]

Under the directorship of William Beveridge, the future architect of Britain's welfare state, the university had won a reputation as a centre of liberal thought, drawing attention for its staged debates between the likes of economist John Maynard Keynes and Austrian-born philosopher Friedrich Hayek, who was himself soon to become an exile from Nazi Germany.

But it was the Jewish political theorist and Fabian Society socialist Harold Laski, whose teaching most attracted the young German, who arrived in London with just "ten Reichsmarks in my pocket".[4]

Marxist historian Ralph Miliband, the father of politician brothers David and Ed Miliband, later recalled the style of Laski's lectures: "He had a glowing faith that youth was generous and alive, eager and enthusiastic and fresh. That by helping young people he was helping the future and bringing nearer that brave world in which he so passionately believed."[5]

Gerngross returned home to begin his legal training, but no sooner had he taken his first law exam than he received his call-up papers. At 10am on Monday 18 June 1939, Rupprecht Paul Gerngross walked into the police headquarters in Munich's *Ettstraße* and was formally signed into Hitler's army. Within weeks, he was in a squadron of horsemen riding into Poland.

There had never been any doubt in Gerngross's mind that he would answer that call; he had long nurtured ambitions to wear the uniform with the scarlet flashes along the seams of his trousers, denoting the rank of officer. But he would do so with a tortured ambiguity.

"I entered into it unwillingly," he said later... "(but) for the Germany that existed before Hitler, that was still there under the brown shroud of the Nazi Party, I was prepared to give my life."[6] His bravery on the battlefield was noted by his superiors and, on November 26 1939, he was awarded the Iron Cross (second class).

As a Reserve Lieutenant for the horse-drawn Infantry Regiment 19, part of the elite 1st Mountain

Division, he joined the siege of Lwow (modern day Lviv in western Ukraine) on the day it began, September 12 1939.

Holed up in a trench, a bullet from a Polish sniper forced him to jump backwards into a rainswept bomb crater. There, to his surprise, was his old Colonel from Steel Helmets days, Adolf Seitz. After much back-slapping and draining of flasks, talk turned to the course of the war. [7]

Poland had been targeted with massive force. No fewer than fifty German divisions smashed their way through its borders on three fronts on September 1. Now with serious resistance crushed, the German commander General Heinz Guderian formally joined up with Hitler's new allies, the Soviet Union, thus sealing Poland's wartime fate.

Already, though, rumours of Nazi atrocities and barbarism were swirling up and down the Eastern Frontline. Rupprecht and his fellow 'old school' officer, heard them with trepidation.

Heinrich Himmler, the architect of the coming Holocaust, had ordered that "only the bare minimum of information" was to be given to the army about the *modus operandi* of the shadowy *Einsatzgruppen* (Task Forces) which followed in the footsteps of the mainstream fighting units.

`The deception was initially successful. Frontline commanders assumed the SS groups following in their wake were rearguard security protecting them against possible revenge attacks. It did not take long for the ugly truth to emerge. In the words of Henning von

Tresckow, who later took part in the 'Valkyrie' plot to assassinate Hitler, the *Einsatzgruppen* were ruthless, autonomous, "state-sanctioned murder squads".[8]

One decorated captain, Axel von dem Bussche-Streithorst - at 24 the same age as Rupprecht – said, after witnessing the mass slaughter of Jews at Dubno Airfield in the Ukraine in 1942, that he regretted not having done the 'honourable thing': taking off his uniform and lining up with the victims.[9] It was witnessing this atrocity, along with reports such as the one in which Lithuanian death squads "danced on the dead bodies" of Jews after beating them to death that would later push him to volunteer to assassinate Hitler.[10]

In November, Eastern Districts Commander in Chief General Johannes Blaskowitz sent Hitler a memo expressing his "utmost concern" at the atrocities and drawing attention to the effect on troops' morale and discipline, following it up with further complaint that the "bloodthirstiness" of the *Einsatzkommando*s was placing an "intolerable burden" on his men and asking for a "new order". "Every soldier feels disgusted and repelled by agents of the Reich," he said. Hitler, rejecting his request, retorted that: "You can't wage war with Salvation Army methods." Six months later, Blaskowitz was dismissed.[11]

By 1940 these mobile killing units were held responsible for 52,000 deaths in Poland, most of them Jews, aristocrats and members of the intelligentsia.[12] Gerngross found the reports shocking, but struggled to believe that the Wehrmacht could possibly be paving the way for such crimes. A few days later, a Polish sniper's bullet provided the confirmation.

Taken to a field hospital in Jaroslaw, 80 miles away, to recover from his wound, he awoke one morning to the sound of gunfire. Who was doing the shooting? As far as he was aware, a ceasefire was in operation.

The sight of people digging in a field would have been commonplace on Polish farmland, had it not been for their loose black clothes fluttering in the wind. Then came the rifle bursts. "From quite close quarters," he said. "I realised I was watching the execution of civilians. Their clothing told me they were Jews... I was seeing what had been spoken of in Nazi language as the 'Final Solution'... it confirmed the deep revulsion I had felt towards the regime in the years before the war."

The scene seared itself into his mind; the helpless dignity of the victims as their payot were shorn in what Gerngross described as a "spiritual torture" and the gratuitous sadism with which they were shown the dead bodies in the open grave before being shot and pushed in. The naked bodies lay in heaps as their still-warm clothes were folded, with energetic efficiency, into neat piles.[13]

Joining troops invading the Soviet Union, once he had recovered, was an experience even less edifying. The commander of his new battalion had all the Jews in a village rounded up and herded into a duckpond. "I will have you baptised," he roared, shooting at them with his pistol so that they were forced to dive under the water and either drown or die from gunshot wounds. [14]

The images returned to haunt him as he lay injured and only half-conscious after a shellblast left him pinned beneath the body of his dying horse and left for dead on the march to Smolensk in the winter of 1941. In the delirium of pain he felt he was "living through" what he imagined to have been the experiences of the Jews he had seen murdered as they, too, had lain dying in their mass grave, "eyes open and waiting for earth to be tipped over them.... and it's over."[15]

Gerngross recovered but the sense of shame never left him. Like Axel von Bussche, he felt his Nazi uniform to be "a stain on his skin". From that point on, he vowed to "undertake everything in my power to defeat 'Hitlerism' entirely."[16]

The Gerngross family (top) beginning their new life in Bavaria in the summer of 1926. Left to right: Rupprecht, Helene, Richard Otto, Richard Gerngross and Barbara. And (below) the health clinic set up by Rupprecht's father in Bad Wiessee. Pictures courtesy of the photo library of Studienwerk deutsches Leben in Ostasien (German Life in East Asia Foundation) reg. nos P7503 and P7054.

3

Gerngross' battle wounds left him "unfit for active service" and in November 1941 he returned to Munich with directions to train fresh recruits in the *Ersatzheer* (Replacement Army).

Munich, the hallowed Bavarian city, which Hitler said he was "bound to by immeasurable love" [1], was outwardly thriving under the Führer's patronage. Expensive renovations and redevelopment had been authorised, and the dictator himself had established his offices in an elegant 19th century mansion, known as the 'Brown House'.

Production lines at the city's factories hummed day and night turning out a vast range of war machinery from field guns to U-boat batteries.

The people of Munich, engaged for half a century in a jealous battle for status with the Prussian capital, Berlin, were gratified by the recognition and the funds that flowed from Hitler's favour. Huge crowds turned out when he made appearances, and in 1941, the year Gerngross returned home, the city laid on a vast Christmas party at which he would preside. Steeped in Nazi ideology, it featured the Teutonic god Odin in place of Father Christmas and a tree with a giant swastika pinned to its topmost branch.[2]

Every schoolday classes began with pupils chorusing 'Heil Hitler' and giving the *Hitlergruß* salute.[3] School prayers and hymns were replaced with Nazi songs and slogans, and anyone wearing the party insignia was to be saluted on the street. Under Hitler's policy of *'Gleichschaltung'* (conformity to the party) every aspect of the city's daily life was watched over and brought into line with Nazi policy.

The Gerngross family, whose medical practice, still run by Richard, was just a short distance from the *Hanselbauer* hotel, where the 1934 'Night of the Long Knives' murders of SA Leader Ernst Röhm and at least 84 others had taken place, could only look on in horror as the city – once a great centre of ideas and free-thinking – descended into slavish adherence.

"The word of the Führer became law,"[4] remembered Rupprecht, with "dead-eyed Nazis", roaming the streets, ready to crush the faintest whiff of dissent. Questions about what was really happening at the 'correction camp' growing daily in size at Dachau, just ten miles down the road were best kept unasked. The choice was stark – accept a life of subjugation or risk the consequences.

Hitler's astonishing hold over the country was initially put down by Gerngross to Goebbel's "witchcraft".[5] Yet he could not help being curious about this unlikely messiah, whose oratory could whip crowds into a boiling frenzy, and whose personal magnetism was felt as keenly by women as men.

Although Hitler permitted himself little time for romance, love of the Führer would drive at least three female disciples – Geli Raubal, Unity Mitford and, eventually, Eva Braun – to suicide.

But seeing him in the flesh for the first time at a Nuremberg parade during his *Reichsarbeitsdienst* (compulsory Reich Labour Service), Gerngross could only feel repulsed by the hunched and crow-like figure on the podium. He "slouched, round-shouldered and stooped while we marched past high-stepping with stiff-legs"[6]... "a parvenu covering his inferiority complex with an outsize trench coat, aping the nobility by clutching a riding crop."[7]

Back in Munich, Rupprecht's disgust deepened and he made the decision to somehow fight back 'from within'.

While serving in Poland he had noticed a small advert in one of the National Services Offices. 'Translators wanted', it read. English was one of the languages needed, along with French; he spoke both fluently.

Interpreters had long held an honourable place in the German military. Now, with so many countries caught up in the conflict, they were needed more than ever – to liaise with people in occupied lands, intercept enemy communications, translate at trials, censor foreign correspondence and, crucially, interrogate prisoners of war.

As the Reich expanded its conquests an even broader range of languages was needed and in 1941 the Wehrmacht ordered each of its twenty or so military districts to set up their own interpreting units.

On November 10 of that year, Gerngross joined Munich's *Dolmetscherkompanie VII* (Wehrmacht Interpreter Company VII), DOLKO for short. He ranked highly, obtaining Level 1 (the topmost level) in English, French and Chinese skills and in just eight months, the 26-year-old was promoted to the rank of captain and took over its command. He started hiring immediately.

His plan was simple but ambitious; he had no say over who arrived on the doorstep of his interpreting unit, clutching their freshly-typed certificates of competence, but he had a free hand over how they were deployed. Thus he could arrange to send the hardcore, committed Nazis to the front, allowing him to secretly train those fighting fit and potentially sympathetic to the cause for his planned rebellion.

The DOLKO served as a perfect disguise for an underground resistance movement. Travel to meet contacts could be authorised under the pretext of seeking out new recruits, and access was granted to all prisoner of war (PoW) camps, where, shortly before the end of the war in mid-March 1945, the Germans were holding 117,000, in the Munich region alone.[8] Where better to get the latest information about what was really happening on the frontline *for themselves*? Information could be exchanged under the camouflage of 'language training sessions'.

The company became steadily more valued as German troops undertook an increasing number of subterfuge missions, such as Operation *Greif*, where the uniforms of dead American and British soldiers were used as disguise to sew confusion. The smallest slip, such as asking an American soldier for 'petrol' instead of 'gas', could mean the difference between life and death. Recognising this rise in their status, General Command placed Gerngross' team under its wing – and effectively left him to organise its work with little interference.

The 280 interpreters in Gerngross's company were an extraordinary collection of different talents and personalities. Among them were intellectuals, professors of art and literature and a man who had developed his language skills as an international hotel thief. There were aristocrats, including two princes – Johann and Stephan – from the wealthy and distinguished House of Arenberg and Guido-Henkel-Donnersmark, a relative of today's Oscar-winning German film director, Florian Henckel von Donnersmark, along with émigrés whose German had been learned while working in bars.[9]

There was a gold medal-winning Olympic athlete, a published poet, an opera singer, a cartoonist known for his unflattering portrayals of Winston Churchill and an artist, whose refusal to join the Nazi party had cost him his professorship. They rubbed shoulders with hairdressers, bakers and even a Benedictine priest who had fought on the Eastern Front and earned what was known in barrack-room parlance as "the Order of the Frozen Flesh" (the *Medaille Winterschlacht im Osten 1941/2*).[10]

They were all soldiers, though, and forced to endure long spells on the front line. They censored the PoWs' post, never daring to let anything go unreported for fear it was a test planted by the Gestapo and monitored activities PoWs conducted in their own languages, from religious services to theatrical performances.[11] Each translator was given the rank of *Sonderführer* (literally, specialist guide) though Gerngross had to admit that, when it came to imposing military discipline on such free-thinking spirits, they were "harder to keep together than a sack of fleas".[12]

Forced, initially, to work in a gloomy, gas-lit school building in the *Versailler Straße* in the east of the city, they rapidly became a close-knit group with a strong sense of camaraderie. Their bewildering range of talents tied them together, and enabled them to pass the evenings making toys for children whose homes had been bombed, smuggling in bottles of wine to make up for the "thin wartime beer".[13]

In this they also proved perfect material for the underground resistance Gerngross was hoping to create. "It was inevitable that among the choice of many men who had mastered a foreign language abroad, you would find people who were far-sighted, people who did not blindly believe and do everything that the National Socialist government ordered them to.... they had seen the world and viewed things in their homeland from a different perspective," he wrote later.[14]

Not everyone was a suitable candidate. Karl Ude, a

young journalist and writer of fawning articles about the regime, was left baffled by the intensive programme of night marches, assault courses and endless hours on the outdoor firing range, and his transfer papers could not arrive soon enough.

He wrote of Gerngross: "He was an army type, who harassed us like young recruits, chasing us over the meadows with war-like tirades and a bilge of barrack-yard phrases as if he was determined to win the war with this little-tested company of translators."[15]

It did not matter in the least to Gerngross that he was considered a harmless eccentric. It all served to deflect suspicion and disguise what he saw as the DOLKO's true purpose, that of a resistance cell. In truth, he barely needed a camouflage; few would have suspected the bespectacled head of a company of translators of plotting to topple the Third Reich.

Conversely, he and his men were becoming ever more skilled at detecting those who might betray *them* – a growing danger as they groped cautiously into hidden corners seeking the 'like-minded'. "In the end," recalled Rupprecht, "you developed an instinct so strong that you could almost *smell* the Nazis."[16]

The company was not alone. Small groups of sympathisers were now mushrooming all over Munich and its surrounding villages. In some of them were people Rupprecht had first met as a schoolboy in the shed at the bottom of his father's garden. The anti-Nazi networks were a mass of intersecting cogs and circles, embracing a broad range of characters and motives ranging from monarchism to Marxism.

Gerngross, whose first rule was: 'meet face to face and commit nothing to paper' was aware of the fragility of this loose-linked resistance. "There was great danger of betrayal. There were no meetings or membership cards, simply friends, those you knew and the like-minded... we were simply 'the ones who knew' but we had great trust in one another."[17]

Colonel Franz Sperr (left): a career officer from the Bavarian army, he was at the centre of a conspiracy in Bavaria to bring down Hitler's National Socialists. He warned Count Claus von Stauffenberg not to go ahead with his plan to assassinate Hitler believing it to be too dangerous, but was sentenced to death for failing to inform the authorities and hanged in Berlin in January 1945. Picture courtesy of the private archive collection of Dr Helmut Moll, Cologne, Germany, author of: "Zeugen für Christus – Das Deutsche Martyrologium des 20. Jahrhunderts". White Rose resistance group member Christoph Probst (top right), who was sentenced to death by guillotine aged 24 in February 1943. His father-in-law was a neighbour of the Gerngross family in Bad Wiessee. (Right) Eva Braun in 1942.

4

Everyone was agreed on a guiding principle: "to achieve the best possible outcome.... putting as few lives at risk as possible and with the least possible bloodshed."[1] So it came as a shock when Franz Geiger, a recent DOLKO recruit, burst into his office one warm July morning waving a leaflet produced by the underground 'White Rose' movement.

Gerngross examined it carefully but not before slamming shut the open window, lest the ensuing conversation be overheard.

The founders of White Rose, Munich University medical students Hans Scholl and his sister, Sophie, were former Hitler Youth members who had turned against the regime after witnessing the mass-murder of Jews on the Eastern front during their service in the Wehrmacht medical corps.

Back in Munich in the summer of 1942, they began producing anti-Nazi pamphlets, denouncing the regime's true character and calling for peaceful resistance. A small network of supporters ensured distribution to other parts of Germany. Geiger, a young actor before the war, knew the owner of the backstreet workshop where the pamphlets were produced. This location and the dissidents behind White Rose were being furiously sought by the Gestapo, itself under intense political pressure to hunt down and destroy any such opposition.

The leaflet delivered by Geiger, was a powerfully-expressed, idealistic call for decent Germans to stand up against the regime, but it left Gerngross unmoved. It would be strategy and pragmatism, he knew, not idealism that would finally end the tyranny. "It's admirable," he told Geiger, "but they are simply putting their lives at risk. In a dictatorship such as this one, amid such tyranny, it's like standing naked in front of a tank."[2]

The Scholls and a fellow student, Christoph Probst, were informed upon and arrested on February 18, found guilty of treason and guillotined four days later at Stadelheim Prison, just outside Munich, where Hitler had, himself, once been a prisoner.

Gerngross took no pleasure in having predicted the likely outcome of the White Rose rebellion, but it reinforced his conviction that a different approach was necessary. "They did all they could within their power to stand up to (the Nazis) but it was dreadful that they achieved so little when they had taken such a terrible risk," he said.

By now other groups were coming to Gerngross with plans he could at least consider. These included smuggling Jewish prisoners out of Dachau and training them to join an uprising. Others – more fanciful – involved money and military force they simply did not have. Still Gerngross took encouragement from the fact that fresh ideas were bubbling all around him. Summoned one morning to the imposing, neo-classical Prinz-Carl-Palais in *Königinstraße*, he was ushered through a set of elegant carved-wood doors and found himself in a stateroom before a group of 'Lords-in-waiting'.[3]

His hosts, monarchists each and every one, explained their view that the best way to stop Hitler was to restore Crown Prince Rupprecht to the Bavarian throne. Driven into exile by the Nazis, the Prince, who had served bravely in the First World War, remained popular with his people and secure in his view that Hitler was insane.[4]

Gerngross politely expressed his scepticism, but the meeting did prove fruitful; among those in the monarchist circle was Colonel Franz Sperr, the last head of the Bavarian legation in Berlin, who would later be executed for his part in the 'Valkyrie' conspiracy. Sperr and Gerngross became great friends.

Bringing down the Third Reich by assassinating the man who was its embodiment had both tantalised and tormented Hitler's opponents ever since November 1939, when a bomb made by carpenter Georg Elser exploded in Munich's *Bürgerbräukeller* missing Hitler by just thirteen minutes.

The idea of a 'lone wolf' attack had crossed Gerngross's own mind when he found himself waiting for the Führer to cross a bridge in Poland to inspect troops. "*We* could do it," he had whispered to a trusted fellow officer as they watched a cavalcade of black

54

Mercedes pull up on the opposite river bank. Hitler's car was yet to be protected with bulletproof glass and armour, and the Führer sat alone, an easy target, alongside his chauffeur *Obersturmbannführer* Erich Kempka.

"Look, you're in charge of anti-tank weaponry, I'm in control of artillery guns. If his car turns and comes over this bridge, we could take him out in the crossfire," Gerngross continued. His companion, staring straight ahead, replied with the cryptic motion of pulling out a dagger.[5]

Gerngross understood. No German soldier of honour could contemplate taking the life of another. So beyond the pale was the idea of a 'stab-in-the-back' even a monster like Hitler was off limits.

But as the horrors mounted, Gerngross's moral inhibitions faded, and when fate held out two further chances, he seized them. In January 1943, he found himself living in a house in the *Böhmerwaldplatz* district of Munich almost directly opposite the studios of Hitler's official photographer, Heinrich Hoffmann. As Gerngross soon discovered, the Führer's frequent visits had less to do with photographic portraits than they did with his attractive, young photography assistant and model Eva Braun.

Eva continued to work there long after Hitler had first asked to be introduced to her as "Herr Wolff" in 1929 when he was 40 and she was 17. She had even stayed on after he bought a villa for her and her sister, Gretl, nearby, though she spent most of her evenings at Hitler's apartment, prompting her to giggle on seeing photographs of British Prime Minister Neville Chamberlain seated on Hitler's sofa; "If only he knew what goings-on that sofa has seen."[6]

While Eva's movements generally followed a routine, Hitler's appearances at the studios were unpredictable, which somewhat complicated Gerngross's calculations of whether he could kill his man with a single sniper's bullet and make good an escape.[7]

From an attic window, he could look out over the studios but only once while he was on 'watch' did the Führer's black Mercedes appear. Gerngross picked up his shotgun, hands sweating as he positioned it on the rim of a small skylight. He was still straining to see the target, finger on the trigger when at that very moment a young mother pushing a pram walked across the driveway, stopping when she noticed who was stood there – and stayed directly in front of the target.[8]

Railing at himself, the heavens and the poor unfortunate woman, who had chanced to pass by, Gerngross was inconsolable at the missed opportunity.

He confided his despair to DOLKO member Lieutenant Leo Heuwing, who, in turn, came up with a bizarre although painstakingly thought-out plan of his own: they would target high-ranking Nazi officials with poison darts. The poison to be used was the blackish, resin produced by tropical plants, known as curare, which had a strychnine-like effect and the deadly projectiles would be fired from blowpipes, like those used by South Americans.[9]

Gerngross' eyes lit up. Not only was it reminiscent of the tales of derring-do from around the world of his boyhood but it had the practical advantage of allowing the assassins to operate in silence, with the chance to slip away before being caught. Further research revealed that supplies of the toxin were kept at Munich's Pharmacological Institute.

But their hopes floundered when they realised the high dosage of curare needed to assure death. Only limited amounts were held in stock, and before they had chance to source further supplies, the institute was destroyed in a bombing raid.

Gerngross was undeterred, indeed, his thirst for action only increased. At night, fantastical, violent visions haunted his dreams – of Hitler lying dead in the street, a gunshot to his temple, blood pouring through the dyed black hair, or his crooked body writhing from the agonies of poison. He would wake, shaking, in a cold sweat: "I am becoming obsessed," he told himself, but still he couldn't drive the desperation to see Hitler dead from his mind.

The day after one such sleepless night, he chanced to meet Sperr on the steps of High Command in Berlin, where he was reporting on the DOLKO's interpreting activities. Sperr's son, Hans Ludwig had just become his newest recruit. The two made for a local bar and Gerngross, knowing his friend was a fellow spirit, confided in him.

Sperr understood. He, too, had long opposed Hitler, and revealed to Gerngross that his apartment in Munich's *Osserstraße* looked directly out over one the Führer occasionally visited – the home of Chief Adjutant Julius Schaub, a fellow veteran of the Beer Hall Putsch. The two men had served jail time together and stayed in regular touch.

The opportunity was not lost on Gerngross. Sperr, a career army officer, recommended a sniper rifle with a telescopic sight, and a plausible escape plan. By the summer of 1944 Gerngross was spending long, hot hours crouched in the Sperrs' attic, once again waiting for Hitler.[10]

He was patient and confident of success, but before the black Mercedes had a chance to purr down *Osserstrasse* again, Claus von Stauffenberg's two briefcase bombs exploded at the Führer's *Wolfsschanze* (Wolf's Lair) headquarters in the forests of northern Poland.

Gerngross was the same age as Stauffenberg, and deeply admired the way in which the young count had united the so-called Kreisau Circle of anti-Hitler conspirators behind his plan. He had known the outline of the plot through Sperr but not its date or time. "The 'Operation Valkyrie' password arrived late in Munich, and was then cancelled. Nothing happened," Gerngross recalled.[11]

Sperr had, in fact, advised Stauffenberg not to go ahead when the two met on June 6 in Bamberg, 140 miles north of Munich, where the young Count had a townhouse. It was six weeks before the bomb was to be detonated and, as they discussed the doomed mission, the first wave of 'D-Day' landings was reaching the Normandy beaches. A skilled tactician,

Sperr had weighed up the pros and cons of the plan, and warned Stauffenberg that it was flawed and fraught with risk. Don't do it, was his verdict. News of the explosion and Stauffenberg's arrest had therefore come as a shock.

It was also the very worst possible outcome – Hitler was injured but alive and thirsting for vengeance. Now the Gestapo would be hunting down anyone with even the faintest connection to any opposition group. Over the next few months around 600 suspects were arrested – few of them directly involved in the plot. The Kaltenbrunner report to Hitler dated 29 November 1944 even named Pope Pius XII as a conspirator.[12] For Gerngross and his men, there was a grim sense of an opportunity vanishing. Every day brought news of fresh arrests.

Evidence that he had met with Stauffenberg was enough to seal Sperr's fate; the kind, cautious 66-year-old along with his wife, Gertrud, was arrested eight days after the bomb was detonated.

But a far greater torment than any the Gestapo could devise for Sperr was that he was "consumed with grief" at not being able to see his son, whom Gerngross had hurriedly sent on an interpreting mission in Yugoslavia for safety. In a moving letter to the young Hans Ludwig, Sperr wrote: "The one thing that has warmed my heart in the weeks of my imprisonment has been the thought of the love... between your mother and myself and our love for you. May you feel swathed in my undying father-love..."[13]

Sperr was brought before the red-robed Judge

Freisler in the Great Hall of the Berlin People's court on January 11 1945 and sentenced to death for failing to inform the authorities of the assassination plans. A devout Catholic, he was deprived of the comfort of last rites as Hitler had expressly forbidden any spiritual consolation, and was executed on January 23, along with nine others.

As a final humiliation in death, his ashes were scattered over a Brandenburg sewage farm. Today the church of Saint George in Munich's *Bogenhausen* district bears a plaque that honours his memory, placed close to the altar where he so often prayed for "a better world".

Almost fifty years after Sperr's death, Gerngross' voice was still shaking with emotion as he recalled the "unspeakable" torture and long, painful death his friend endured to save the lives of others such as himself. "I owe my life to him and to his wife because neither they, nor any of the others, *ever* betrayed us."[14]

Hitler had apparently planned to give the 'traitors' great show trials, with full media coverage, but as they lined up in court and began speaking movingly of how they had wanted, as one put it, to "save Germany from indescribable misery.... and only hope that someone else will succeed," he thought better of it and banned any trial reporting.[15]

There would be no martyrs and there would be no "honourable bullet". They were to be "hanged like cattle"; strung by thin, hemp cord, from specially-erected meat hooks in Berlin's Plötzensee Prison with the result that death could take as long as twenty minutes.[16]

Gerngross quickly found a way around the news blackout. He knew that Bavaria's *Reichstatthalter* (Reich Governor) Franz Ritter von Epp would receive the trial transcripts and, with the help of the governor's Wehrmacht liaison officer, Major Günther Caracciola-Delbrück, collected copies from the "lion's den" of Epp's antechamber on the *Prinzregentenstraße*.

Reading the transcripts, an experience Gerngross described as "a real shock, like having cold water poured over us," filled them with despair. "We felt doomed, lost courage and became embittered," Gerngross recalled.[17]

Eventually, the gloom lifted and they drew inspiration from the last words of encouragement to Stauffenberg from his friend and courageous Hitler opponent, Henning von Tresckow: "Even if it (the assassination) fails, we must take action... For the practical purpose no longer matters; what is important now is that the German resistance movement must take the plunge before the eyes of the world and of history.... nothing else matters."[18]

By the time the thin, hemp cord was placed around Sperr's neck on the ill-fated Sunday morning of January 23 1945, they had shaken off their despair and pledged to honour his memory by continuing their struggle because "nothing else matters".

General Walter von Unruh pictured (left) as a major in World War I, dubbed the "hero-snatcher" after Hitler commissioned him to scour military and civilian offices for manpower to fill ever-widening gaps on the Eastern Front. Gerngross said: "He took people, even if they had not had any training and were likely to be shot. It was a disaster to select troops in this way." (Interview: Museum of the House of Bavarian History, 3 p.11). (Right) Olympic bobsleigh champion Lorenz Nieberl, who was one of Gerngross' translators. Their fastest cycle courier, the FAB relied on him to deliver urgent messages. The 26-year-old's top-speed despatches helped saved lives on the night of the rebellion but Gerngross feared he would be arrested for cycling illegally along the motorway.

5

With the failure of the plot and Sperr's execution, Gerngross' hopes of mass resistance sank, and his supporters struggled to maintain morale. Adding to their despair was the whipped-up, popular *Schadenfreude* at the deaths of the 'traitors'. All around them people rejoiced at the Führer's survival.

The scenes of jubilation seemed detached from the reality of the Reich's floundering war effort. The Soviet Red Army was moving in from the East and the Allied forces from the West. More and more German families were hearing of the deaths of loved ones. Gerngross wondered how it was possible, in the face of all these setbacks, for people to be cheering "the only man who could stave off possible disaster.....Adolf Hitler".[1]

To mark the 12th anniversary of his coming to power, on January 30 1945, the Führer made a thunderously defiant speech calling on the German people to "do their duty to the last" and for even the "sick and the weak to work with their last strength."[2] The same day brought news of the deaths of 9,400 German evacuees when the *Wilhelm Gustloff* sank after being torpedoed by a Soviet submarine.

It seemed to Gerngross that the worse things became, the more blindly and furiously the Nazis fought on. Ordinary people appeared cowed and fatalistic, and there was little criticism of how the war was being conducted or of the high-ranking officers, still posturing as mighty conquerors. Yet an unmistakable whiff of delusion, even decadence, hung in the air. Nazi dignitaries no longer bothered to conceal their drunkenness in public, staggering into their chauffeured cars from a favoured 'drinking den' beneath the *Führerbau* (the Führer's building – today Munich's University of Performing Arts) in the *Arcissstraße*.[3]

Prominent among these was the corpulent SS Brigadier General Christian Weber. A former pub-bouncer, beer-hall thug and braggart, Weber was best known for the notorious brothel he ran in the city's *Senerfeldstraße*. Corrupt even by Nazi standards, he used his position as city councillor to line his pockets through the 'Aryanisation'" (confiscation) of Jewish wealth and property.

He lived in a grand apartment in the *Residenz Palace,* formerly the home of Bavarian kings, dressed flamboyantly and fawningly copied Hitler's habit of carrying a dog whip.[4]

"It made us feel so bitter (that) when we were having to sacrifice, and part with so much that was dear to us," wrote Gerngross. "...Everyone knew how high the losses at the Front were... soldiers died, yet Nazis celebrated." He felt the 'drip of disgust' at the losses suffered by his Jewish friends when he spotted his prized BMW Dixi car in a party official's garage. It had been officially sequestered for the 'war effort' supposedly because its steel was needed for munitions. He was also sceptical about the pile of fur coats collected at his barracks after rich women were pressed to 'do their bit' and donate them to soldiers freezing to death in the Russian winter.[5]

On occasion he would feel a flicker of hope at overhearing people talk of "putting an end to it all" only to discover that they did not mean ending Hitler's tyranny but joining the thousands (the exact numbers are not known) of those committing suicide. Prussic acid was most commonly used.[6]

There were a few attempts to lift the gloom. Audiences still laughed uproariously at shows performed by the Nazi comic Weiß Ferdl (real name Ferdinand Weisheitinger) in the Platzl Square theatre. Ferdl would open his act by marching onstage shouting 'Heil' with his right arm outstretched only to pause in mock confusion saying: "Oh, Goddamn, I've forgotten the name again."

Gerngross saw this as a "safety valve where people could let off steam… although we knew in truth he probably had a good relationship with the Propaganda Ministry because he told jokes that would have put others into concentration camps,"[7]

By Christmas 1944, over not-so-festive drinks with Caracciola-Delbrück, Gerngross was increasingly restless. The conversation turned to Sperr, soon to take his last steps to the gallows, and the condemned man's belief that an uprising in a totalitarian state such as Nazi Germany could succeed only with a 'helping hand from outside' – specifically the Allied forces.[8]

Such help no longer seemed beyond the bounds of reality. By January the Red Army was bearing down on the heartlands of East Prussia while the Western Allies were sweeping through France and the Low Countries. A final reckoning could not be far away.

Gerngross had drawn up a new plan, taking Sperr's advice into account but also drawing on lessons learned from Stauffenberg's failure. The Valkyrie plotters came from a privileged elite; Gerngross' movement would draw on a wider range of experienced middle and lower-ranking officers.

The extraordinary new security measures around the Führer – no one was now allowed in his presence carrying a gun - meant the chances of a successful assassination were remote. Rather than waste resources on an unlikely outcome, the new strategy would be to trigger an uprising in Bavaria while preparing a path for the liberation forces approaching from the West.

The first stage, explained Rupprecht, would be to kidnap or kill three top Nazis holding power in Munich and seize control of the two radio stations covering the Munich area, to announce that an anti-Hitler movement had assumed power. Then to stoke a wider rebellion by urging the population to overthrow the local Nazi establishment. They would have everything in place for a post-Hitler administration, even drawing up a plan for an interim government written around the needs of ordinary people.

Caracciola-Delbrück was as enthused as he was horrified. "I believe we can do this if we limit it to our Bavarian homeland," Gerngross reassured him. "We just follow our conscience and stay committed... but I feel freed from the belief that we have to kill Hitler... Satan, himself, protects him, like a guardian angel."[9]

Gerngross even had a new name for his group: *Freiheitsaktion Bayern* (the Freedom Action of Bavaria – FAB for short). *"Freedom,"* he explained, "because freedom is what we would have if we can rid ourselves of National Socialism, *'Action'* because our aim is the forceful removal of the regime from all areas of society, not just to become an anti-Hitler 'debating club, losing ourselves in endless discussion circles'.... and *Bavaria* because the attempt to find a solution for the whole country has failed, and we can only organise an effective resistance on a smaller scale."[10]

But clasping the 'helping hand from outside' came with complications. They had no contacts in the Allied forces, and the British had been extremely distrustful of the "German Resistance" since the notorious Venlo incident in 1939 when two British intelligence agents were lured into a deadly ambush in the Dutch town by one of Himmler's top spies claiming to be part of a plot to kill Hitler.

In one of the worst cases of cynicism, the British historian and Foreign Office mandarin Sir John Wheeler-Bennett even suggested in its wake that the Gestapo and SS were doing the Allies "an appreciable service" by removing many who would "pose as 'Good Germans' after the war and cause us endless embarrassments."[11]

Stauffenberg's attempt on Hitler's life had failed to prompt any interest or support from the Americans. Goebbels appeared to have convinced people the Russians were "Bolshevik Beasts" hell-bent on revenge for atrocities wrought by SS troops in their lands. The plotters were very much alone.

Seizing control of radio stations had formed part of the doomed Valkyrie plot. An elite reserve brigade got as far as capturing two Berlin radio stations as well as the main broadcasting centre, but a lack of technical know-how prevented them from halting transmissions by Goebbels. They had relied on the station manager who said the frequency had been shut down, when it hadn't.

This enabled a series of announcements to go out from Führer headquarters describing the bomb attack but defiantly proclaiming that Hitler had escaped injury and "resumed his work" immediately.

It meant that few Germans even knew of Stauffenberg's effort until it was all over. Gerngross was not going to make the same costly mistake – they would use technicians with specialist radio knowledge.[12]

Both men agreed that they, as unknowns, would never be trusted by the Allies; they needed someone well-known and widely respected to be the uprising's public figurehead. Caracciola-Delbrück felt sure the man he had served loyally for so many years,

Governor Franz Ritter von Epp, would step up for the role. Epp's disdain for the Nazis was well-known. He had been mocked for his Catholic piety by the young lions in Hitler's pride, who dubbed him the "Mother-of-God's General".[13] Gauleiter Paul Giesler had sought his removal since 1943. It was a wish Hitler did not grant him but not for the reason he thought.

It was true that Epp had been one of the Führer's earliest supporters. When Hitler needed a newspaper in 1920 he obligingly paid some 60,000 Paper Marks, thought to have come from secret army funds, to purchase the *Völkischer Beobachter* for the NSDAP. By 1921 Hitler was the publication's sole owner and it had become a Nazi mouthpiece.

But whilst prizing loyalty above all, Hitler showed none and when Epp tried to warn him, once too often, against drastic anti-semitism and anti-Catholic measures, Hitler marked him out as 'suspect'. He kept him close but powerless, delivering the snub of making him the only governor not to be made a Gauleiter, instead appointing hard-line Giesler, whose faithfulness was ferocious, to keep a close eye on him.[14]

Giesler promptly put Epp under the surveillance of the SS, assiduously sweeping up any crumb of dissent around the elderly General and delivering it triumphantly to Hitler's inner circle. Goebbels recorded uneasily in his diary in August 1943 that Giesler had told him Epp, among others, was "going in search of peace".[15]

But despite the close SS-watch put on Epp,

astonishingly, reaching the ears of US intelligence spies, [16] it was *not* known to members of the FAB. They saw Epp simply as a calm, dignified figure, popular with the people of Munich, who remembered him crushing a shortlived communist coup in 1919. Caracciola-Delbrück thought the 76-year-old's military prominence, would make him a good negotiator when the Allies arrived.

The plan was now broadly agreed. The bigger problem was how to put it into action in the face of increasingly desperate and panic-stricken measures being taken by the regime.

Himmler had recently revived the notion of *Sippenhaft* ("blood guilt"), effectively meaning that if anyone was found guilty of a crime against the state, their family and relatives would be executed along with them. He claimed, fancifully, that it had once been a legal principle of the Germanic peoples to punish the families of those who betrayed the tribe. Few – however much they longed to be rid of the Nazis – wished to see their wives, children, siblings, even grandparents hanged. As Gerngross noted: "Nearly every one of us was a father."

Hitler further decreed in March that any soldier had the right to shoot another for breach of the faith, and on April 3 it was proclaimed that in any house displaying a white flag, all the males would be shot. Then, on April 20, his 56th birthday, Hitler strengthened the powers of his 40 or so Gauleiters by making them Reich Defence Commissars, effectively transferring almost total control of Reich regions into their hands.

By now almost an entire generation of younger people had undergone Nazi indoctrination, and older people were too demoralised by poverty to think of anything other than the struggle to get through each day. And there remained many whose loyalty to the party remained immovable; Hitler, wreathed in Goebbels' intoxicating propaganda, still held them in his thrall.

New accommodation arrangements left members of the Gauleiter's personal *Volkssturm* troops scattered in army barracks across the city. These ominously named *"zur besonderen Verwendung"* (for special purposes) guards acted as Giesler's "eyes and ears". They were "elite, fit long-serving soldiers vetted for their National Socialist convictions", who wore an armband with "Der Gauleiter" written on it and had superior weapons," Gerngross recalled. "One of these companies was even housed in my barracks... even though there was sufficient barrack space. No one had anything to do with them.[17]

To Gerngross and his men, it seemed as if the system was being "superproofed" against opposition. Everyone, everywhere, was being monitored every moment of the day. The strain of working covertly with ever-diminishing options was, he noted: "unbearable... like living your life with one foot in prison, always with the knowledge of what awaited us. We knew from the July 20 (Valkyrie) plotters what would happen to us [if caught]."[18]

Gerngross held steadfastly to his strategy of

limiting cells of members to no more than five – only he and Leiling would have an overview. Those taking part in the rebellion would be kept in the dark until the night of the rebellion: "We only revealed the tasks on the evening of the uprising and even then some wondered whether it was too early in case someone informed on us and betrayed us."[19]

Leiling knew betrayal was a real possibility and fretted for the men's safety but Gerngross was convinced that, in this way, they could keep their planned coup safe from prying eyes.

Only two troubling moments shook his confidence. The first was when the Prussian Infantry General Walter von Unruh strode into his office unannounced. He had been specially commissioned by Hitler to fill ever-widening manpower gaps on the frontline by probing every corner of every military office for men whose jobs he could declare 'surplus' so that they could fight.[20]

Gerngross felt his interpreters should be exempt because they fulfilled vital roles. He had fended off past attempts to 'steal back' his hard core resistance fighters for the front by listing them as proficient in desperately needed 'shortage languages' but had not reckoned with the unwearied persistence of the dapper, beady-eyed general, who had been personally commissioned by Hitler to delve into the dark corners of every Reich army office to seek out draft-age manpower.

Gerngross, himself, was subjected to an intense interrogation, then forced to summon the entire company under Unruh's scrutinising gaze. The general's eyes lighted on Olympic athlete Sergeant Lorenz Nieberl.

Gerngross breathed in sharply. Nieberl, his fastest cycle courier, earmarked for a vital role in delivering messages at top speed on the night of the rebellion, spoke Russian but it was not a sufficiently rare enough language to keep him out of Unruh's determined clutches.

'What do you do in the company?' Unruh asked. Nieberl's quick-thinking mind did not desert him and he told the General he spoke 'Georgian'. Eyeing him suspiciously, Unruh asked him. 'So what, then, is the Georgian word for 'gasmask'? Nieberl stared at the general as if truly astonished that he did not know and replied confidently: *"Urskrewinski!"*. Realising there was probably no such word but helpless to state otherwise, Unruh muttered: 'Good, the man can stay,' and departed swiftly.[21]

Everyone breathed a sigh of relief, but it was not long before a second incident set alarm bells ringing that they might be under surveillance. The unexpected arrival of a new member at the DOLKO from an interpreters' unit in Salzburg aroused Gerngross' suspicions. "He stood to attention, his heels clattering together with a deafening noise... I thought to myself, he does that just like the SA," he recalled. Checks soon revealed he was a full-time NSDAP official.

Confronting the man over his blatant 'lies', a furious Gerngross stripped him of his interpreter's *Sonderführer* rank and despatched him immediately

73

to the Eastern Front. The move alarmed his fellow DOLKO members who feared the man might have been a Gestapo spy. One commented nervously: "You treated him harshly. Let us hope nothing comes of it."

Gerngross reassured him it wouldn't but learned later the man had submitted a report to General Command about the 'counter-revolutionary spirit' that was rife in Gerngross' company. It was filed in a thickening dossier.

But soon there was no time left to agonise further; an order issued from Hitler's bunker on March 19 was to shock them all into action. The 'Nero' decree, officially the *Befehl betreffend Zerstörungsmaßnahmen* (Demolitions on Reich Territory Decree) and named after the Roman Emperor, who allegedly danced while Rome burned, put into law Hitler's "scorched earth" policy.

It was a suicidal strategy, mandating the destruction of any 'material assets' the occupying forces could use, including food, water, electricity, factories, railways and bridges. As American war correspondent William Shirer wrote: "Germany was to be made one vast wasteland. Nothing was to be left with which the German people might somehow survive their defeat."[22]

At the same time, after years of being largely protected from air-raids by its distance from Britain, Munich had begun to be pounded by Allied bombing raids, with the city being identified as "the last heaping great nest of Nazis" and warnings that nothing would be spared in efforts to "smoke out its

74

filthy brood".[23]

By April 1945, the bombing missions had killed 6,632 people and wounded 15,800; more than 80,000 homes were destroyed and swathes of the city had been pummelled into an estimated 10 million cubic metres of rubble,[24] enough to fill more than a hundred Royal Albert Halls.

This left Munich facing its own 'war on two fronts'. Except that one threat came from the outside, the other from within. To Gerngross, the idea of the Nazis finishing off all that the Allies had not yet succeeded in destroying, was nothing short of an "act of sadism" by Hitler against his own people. "We were determined that devastation and destruction would not usher in the new beginnings of life that was to come after the Nazi-era."[25]

In the weeks before the assassination attempt, Stauffenberg had muttered: 'We must save Germany.' Someone had to pick up the baton. It was too late to save the rest of the country but Gerngross hoped to, at least, save Munich and the near half a million people still living there, from one final, futile act of destruction.

Lt. General Karl Kriebel, one of the generals who drummed Valkyrie plotters out of the army, depriving them of the legal protections of a court-martial. In a ruse to obtain accurate reports of the fighting at the front, Gerngross offered the general a 'personalised' news service staffed by his military translators gathering information from all over the world. He took the bait.

6

Easter Sunday, April 1 1945, found the men of FAB in a state of anxious uncertainty. The war was clearly lost, but which invading army would advance furthest and fastest and what would be the consequences for Munich?

Away to the north, rival Red Army Marshals Ivan Koniev and Georgii Zhukov were competing for the big prize of Berlin, where the besieged Führer was now trapped in an underground bunker.

'Second prize' Munich was initially rejected by the hard-charging US General George Patton. In a rare moment of agreement with Britain's Field Marshal Bernard Montgomery, he urged a daring, high-speed advance on the capital, but both were overruled by Allied commander Dwight Eisenhower, who feared massive losses. Patton bitterly wrote to his wife, Beatrice: "I don't see much future for me in this war. There are too many safety-first people running it." [1]

Somewhat reluctantly, Patton turned his guns south-eastwards towards the Bavarian plains. Meanwhile, creeping through the Reich's southern underbelly, the Red Army had reached Vienna, only

270 miles to the east.

Gerngross and his men were working hard to track the movements of the approaching armies, but the continuing onslaught of Goebbel's delusional propaganda made reliable information hard to come by. He spent a fretful and distracted Easter Sunday lunch with his parents discussing the latest complication. His wife Brigitte was now pregnant with their second child. There were doubts she could escape *Sippenhaft* by travelling 40 miles to a remote mountain shepherd's hut in the Innsbruck Alps with a 19-month-old toddler in tow.

Nothing appeared certain. The Western Allies had slowed their advance to allow the Red Army to take Berlin unhindered. What other strategic calculations might come into play? At a FAB meeting, late in the night and lubricated by stiff drink, Gerngross came up with an idea. He would seek out the necessary information at the very top of the command chain - even if it meant putting his head "into the lion's jaws".

Goebbels had a personal 'hotline' to the regional Gauleiters. It would ring at precisely midday and, after voice verification, the *Reichsminister* would list the selectively-edited information he wanted people to hear. The Gauleiters would be left in no doubt as to what should, and should not, be reported.

With the help of Caracciola-Delbrück and some of the technical specialists, who had joined the FAB, Gerngross would set up a listening device to tap the calls. Not only did this audacious plan work, it gave the plotters a secret thrill to know that the arch-controller, notorious for his iron grip on communications throughout the Reich, was laying bare the details of what Gerngross called his "Nazi-narcosis", unaware that his very own telephone line was being tapped.[2] They felt they were turning the tables - at last.

A second stage of the plan proved equally successful. Feigning concern that Munich's Commander, Lieutenant General Karl Kriebel, was not sent detailed reports of enemy movements or the latest situation at the front and had to rely on newspapers, Gerngross used a routine visit to make a suggestion: "If you were to get the finest radios with the best reach in here," he told the general, "I could set my interpreters to work and you would have news from all over the world much earlier."

Kriebel took the bait - delighted at the prospect of having his own enemy monitoring service that would bring him news ahead of other generals. Within days, a team of interpreters was installed in a room next to his office in a requisitioned Jesuit training college in the north of the city.[3]

Now FAB had undreamt-of access to foreign newspaper and radio station coverage. There was no more need to huddle in attics around a cheap, Goebbels-issue *Volksempfänger* (People's Receiver) radio with its bright orange "Wartime Special Penal Code" warning users that being caught with the dial in the wrong position could mean death.

General Kriebel was no doubt astonished at the diligence of Gerngross' interpreters as they worked around the clock, transcribing and summarising every speech, political commentary and battlefield despatch they could find. For the translators, grateful as they were for the information, it was a painful experience to learn for the first time how Germany was viewed by an aggrieved world.

Soon the uncensored news they had access to meant the detail of their war charts rivalled those in Hitler's map room, and by contrasting what they now knew to be true with what they were being told, they could see clearly the scale of the misinformation being peddled to the German people.[4]

The FAB's three main figures - Genrgross, Otto-Heinrich Leiling and Leo Heuwing – met almost daily at Leiling's flat. They were always careful to disguise these visits as social occasions, but once through the door, before their talks began, they would heap cushions and blankets over the telephone and its wiring praying that this 'sound insulation' would keep them safe from bugs and the suspicious ears listening in.[5]

Numerous drafts of plans ended up on the stove fire, mostly because the three men realised they could not be achieved with FAB's modest military resources. But on April 6, there came a breakthrough in the form of a new recruit - Major Alois Braun, the commander of a tank unit in Freising, a town just over 20 miles north-east of Munich.

Braun, like Gerngross, had been transferred to the replacement army after being wounded. He had around 2,000 men[5], divided into 15 companies, under his charge in the Panzer-Ersatz-Abteilung 17 and at a first meeting, offered to contribute several *Hetzer Jagdpanzers* (light tank destroyers) and a "significant number" of soldiers, to protect the seized radio stations from SS units.[6] His only condition was that the Americans must agree to call off all bombing raids that night.[7] In return, his men would then open up a corridor to allow their troops safe entry into the city.

With these reinforcements, Grengross reckoned to finally have the military strength needed to stage the coup, and hold the city for up to six hours. Although a non-combat unit, the translators had spent months quietly building up a stock of weapons – many originating from wounded soldiers, and smuggled out by hospital sympathisers.[8]

Another undercover operation secured the escape of a small number of Allied PoWs from *Stalag VII-A* at Moosburg, north of Munich. Smuggled out in Red Cross ambulances or local supply vans, these French, British and American prisoners were given false identity papers, hidden in the workshop of car mechanic Georg Rödter in Munich's *Schwabing* district, and lined up as liaison officers with the approaching forces.

Additional plans were made to support the FAB's 'reliable people' at Dachau, by smuggling weapons to them so that the prisoners could arm themselves and join the uprising when the time came,[9] preventing the SS from herding its 32,000 internees south across the Alps on a 'death-march'.

Timing was the hardest decision Gerngross faced.

As the German frontline crumbled, Munich was filling up with battle-hardened Nazis heading south to defend Hitler's 'Alpine Fortress'. This imaginary redoubt, stretching from southern Bavaria, across Austria to northern Italy had been conceived by Himmler in the seemingly impossible circumstance of defeat. Although Hitler never fully endorsed the plan, and many of its supposed features – including food stores and fortifications – never existed, many troops believed it would be the site of a heroic last stand where – as the Führer had ordered – they would fight to the "last drop of blood".

For his part, Gerngross still clung to the principle of keeping bloodshed to a minimum. This would require a precise calculation. Somehow he had to strike *after* the Allied Forces had crossed the Danube and were no more than a "safe day's march away" but *before* Munich became overrun with what he calls 'war-upholding' Nazis looking for martyrdom. "There was great danger if we moved too early but there was also great danger if we moved too late," Gerngross recalled. "It was like having the Sword of Damocles hanging over us..."[10]

The radio station at Ismaning, just outside the town of Erding, north of Munich, one of two seized by the FAB on the night of the uprising. It is pictured here in the 1930s. Photograph courtesy of the Historical Archive of the Bavarian Broadcasting Corporation (BR, Historisches Archiv, F18.7). (top) The transmission control panel inside from where the FAB broadcasts were made. Photograph courtesy of the Historical Archive of the Bavarian Broadcasting Corporation (BR, Historisches Archiv, F18.10).

7

On April 20, Nuremberg, the Temple City of Nazism, home of the Führer's great rallies, and less than a hundred miles from Munich, fell to the US Seventh Army, and the American flag was hoisted in the soon-to-be renamed Adolf-Hitler Square. It was the Führer's 56th birthday

As if in a parallel universe, the crowds in Berlin still turned out to mark the occasion with all the usual fervour, and an impressive display of the latest Wehrmacht weaponry and equipment was set up in the Reich Chancellery for his inspection.[1]

Hitler, though, appeared only in the chancellery garden where, seemingly stooped and jowly-faced, he awarded Iron Crosses to members of the Hitler Youth. Goebbels made a morale-raising speech reassuring people that "fate will give him [Hitler] and his people the laurel wreath of victory" and instructions were issued for the enemy to be "halted once and for all" at the banks of the Danube and the Iller, two of the rivers that curve protectively around the southern corner of Germany.[2]

But Nuremberg lay devastated after a five-day

battle in which American troops met fierce resistance. When 30 men from the city, seeing their situation as hopeless, had approached the enemy waving white flags, they were machine-gunned to death by their own side.[3] Fearful of events being repeated in Munich, the FAB were now in urgent need of a 'helping hand'.

Gerngross and Braun despatched five FAB envoys across combat lines to the northern Bavarian town of *Neudorf*, where troops from the US Seventh Army led by Lt. General Alexander Patch had set up camp on the banks of the Danube.

Two injured officers, unable to play an active part in the uprising, were keen to undertake the mission and, despite their reservations, Gerngross and Braun despatched Oberleutnant Leo Mahlke, 31, who had lost an arm and Leutnant Jakob Feller, 28, who had lost an eye, under cover of night on the 60-mile trek, heavily disguised. As a back-up, two American PoWs: US air force pilot Sidney Leigh[4] and First Lieutenant Bernard McNamara travelled on a different route to *Neudorf* in a Red Cross ambulance driven by a young *Gefreite* [lance corporal] with "must be urgently interrogated" papers to get them through Nazi checkpoints.[5]

Mahlke and Feller arrived first; US Army records show that the two men were arrested at 2pm on April 24, wandering around the camp outskirts by bemused officials who were suspicious of their offer of the peaceful surrender of the area of Munich covered by Braun's unit.[6]

But US military intelligence, which was monitoring

the situation closely from Switzerland, took what the men were saying far more seriously, especially when they produced maps outlining Hitler's planned defence of Munich, including details of five major bridges to be booby-trapped or destroyed and small local airfields where the FAB could provide cover for planes to land.

Their story matched up with improbable radio messages Allied communications had been receiving, transmitted from a car mechanic's workshop in Munich and, until now, ignored.

The proposal of safe entry into Munich, shielded from SS-units if the Allies halted bombing raids was listened to. All the FAB men needed, the envoys said, was for US planes to signal their agreement to the plan by dropping five flares directly over Braun's 17th Panzer base at Freising, north of Munich. They even produced a sketch plan showing the exact location of the barracks.[7]

That very night, plane after plane from the US Airforce swept low over Freising, and families cowering in their cellars strained their ears for the whistle of falling bombs. Not a single one was dropped. Instead, to the delight of FAB members, the sky lit up with five of the blinding flares normally used to pinpoint night-time targets. They shone from such a height and were so dazzlingly bright, the Germans dubbed them sarcastically "Christmas trees".[8]   It would be the only time they ever brought a gift of peace.

Gerngross was understandably relieved. "I took it

as an OK," he wrote; he was sure Lt Gen. Patch understood what he was planning and would enter Munich as soon as the FAB had the city under control.[9]

A defiant new codeword that Munich's citizens would recognise when it was broadcast from the captured radio stations was chosen. Now the signal would be '*Fasanenjagd* ' ('pheasant shoot'). 'Golden pheasants' was a mocking term for the high-ranking Nazis who strutted around, with the golden party badge and colourful insignia on their puffed-out chests. Gerngross was confident that even people "in the remotest dwelling", would understand precisely which quarry they should shoot.[10]

As the hours went by, his high excitement was tempered by fear that the timing might be wrong. "Giving the crucial order [to launch the action] and issuing the password was a burden that lay with me alone," he recalled.[11] Fearing the Gestapo's night-time knock, he took to sleeping with a rope under the bed so that he could escape through the nearest window if it came.[12]

A few weeks earlier, unable to sleep, he had switched on the radio. What he heard made him sit bolt upright in bed. Amid the static hissing and clicking of the Nazi jamming efforts, he heard a voice speaking his very own words back to him.

A young man called Hagedorn from an underground German resistance movement was urging a friend to join him in "overcoming the Nazis, the true enemy of Germany" by negotiating a peaceful surrender to the Allies.

"Together, we will hang out the white flag of freedom," Hagedorn reassured his reluctant friend. "Peaceful surrender is the only way, but do not make plans involving German generals....we don't want one of these officers' affairs like July 20 (the 'Valkyrie' plot)... The uprising must come from the people. As if addressing Gerngross, personally, he assured him: "Peace is on the way, but it is not time to act yet... The Allies must come nearer..."

Gerngross was, in fact, listening to a radio 'soap opera' that was Allied propaganda designed to turn ordinary Germans against their Nazi masters, but it eerily echoed his own words and thoughts. *Hagedorn* told the story of a group of young resistance fighters trying to save their city from destruction. It was based on information US intelligence workers had received from Switzerland about "a potentially revolutionary group, somewhere in Bavaria, probably Munich, small in number but highly disciplined, composed partly of civilians and partly of a specialised army unit."[13]

Listeners were invited to believe someone was daring to broadcast anti-Nazi resistance on German soil. In reality, the programme was coming from a disused warehouse fifty miles outside London via a British shortwave radio station and, later, the British black propaganda broadcaster *Soldatensender West*.[14]

The first of the ten-minute broadcasts went out over the airwaves on February 26 and struck a chord with German listeners, who managed to catch most episodes despite the efforts of the Nazi jammers. In her book *Freiheitsaktion Bayern*, German historian Veronika Diem believes the project may have had Munich's FAB specifically in mind when they scripted the plot of *Hagedorn* and timed its broadcast to help them know when would be the best time to launch the uprising. The story was "probably invented.... on the basis of information coming from Munich," she concludes and "could have had an influence on when the uprising was started."[15]

After the war the US intelligence agency admitted having penetrated Germany with more than 100 spying missions over the last eight months of the war, including several to Munich, to gather information, including the strength of Nazi control over the civilian population.[16] Gerngross and two other men told US officials in an interview that they were among those who had listened to Hagedorn and, though the waveband was hard to get, said the story had "deeply influenced those who *did* hear him.... There was an uncanny parallel between our ideas and those of Hagedorn... Many times we said to each other: 'What Hagedorn says is exactly what we think'."[17]

On April 25, Hitler's Reich splintered into two as American troops advancing from the West and Soviet troops moving in from the East met at the Saxon town of Torgau, just over 300 miles north of Munich. Berlin was completely encircled but still the Wehrmacht soldiers fought on, losing around 350,000 men per month.[18] It *had* to end.

The long wait almost over, Gerngross travelled to *Bad Wiessee* to rehearse the arrangements for his wife

Brigitte's journey to the shepherd's hut on the Guffert mountain in the Tyrol, where she would be safe. Shielded from above by dense mountain pines, it was also impossible to approach from below without detection.[19]

He found the house unusually locked and bolted from within and, inside, his wife in a state of tearful agitation. A shadowy figure had been spotted lurking outside the house late in the evening and she was convinced a man had followed her during the day. Gerngross lay in wait and discovered it was a sergeant who, on paper, was a member of the DOLKO unit but by 'command order' had been engaged in duties elsewhere.

Catching sight of Gerngross, the man moved quickly out of sight in the direction of the opposite shore of the lake. "He had been staking out my house and... you had to think of it, on the other side of the lake was the house owned by Himmler."[20]

Gerngross hid his own sense of foreboding to calm Brigitte, suggesting they took a lakeside stroll. The beer gardens had opened for the Summer and women in bright-coloured *dirndls* were moving between customers but Gerngross felt a shiver of fear. The tiny lakeside resort seemed suddenly so full of cloud and gloom.... and Nazi uniforms. It might have been a premonition. He was, in fact, standing not far from the spot where, days later, one of his closest friends would suffer fatal wounds in a hail of SS bullets.

He left without saying goodbye to his parents, unable to witness his mother's attempt at putting a brave face on things - "I could not bear to see the uncried tears in my mother's eyes – it would have been impossible to keep hidden from her what would happen in the next few days" - and headed back to Munich.[21]

Until now, the FAB leaders had been careful to write nothing down - not a timetable, not a list, not a single order. With one exception. Gerngross had assured Leiling that the carefully-worded plan they had drawn up for Bavaria's post-war future was stored 'in a very safe place'. He didn't say where.

Leiling was a lawyer, whose professional instinct was to keep written copies of everything, and he had struggled at first with this concept. Eventually, he had trained himself to memorise the names and contact details of every FAB member. He was relieved, though, when all the information in his head could finally be dictated to their "champion-typist" – a trusted war widow.

Having recited the last telephone number, he turned to Gerngross: "Your turn, now!", then watched, astonished, as Gerngross, heaving his outsize army boots onto a chair, mounted a table, and began grappling with the large, imposing portrait of Hitler that hung over the fireplace. Unhooking it, he turned the frame around triumphantly to reveal their carefully thought-out conclusions, ten points summing up how Bavaria should be governed, written neatly on the back. Both men laughed uproariously and even the secretary agreed it would have been the last place anyone would have looked. For once, the

91

wretched so-called *Führerliebe* had helped them.[22]

Gerngross had always expected some members who had signed up to his plan to waver, but struggled to hide his frustration with the fainthearts who dropped out at the last moment saying 'Oh, but it could take *days* for the Americans to get here!'[23]

Even those who liked to quote the wartime mantra: *"Lieber ein Ende mit Schrecken als ein Schrecken ohne Ende."*(Better an end with horror than horror without end) found their courage failing when told it was time to act.

Gerngross concedes that they all felt tempted when they heard people say: 'But once the Americans arrive, it's all over, anyway - why risk your neck at the last minute for Christ's sake?'[24] But he knew action would still be needed, and in accepting responsibility for it, he found he was not alone. On the night of the uprising he could count on 440 men ready to battle with him. "We wanted to clearly show that there was a real resistance movement inside Germany."[25]

Some stepped up to their missions with immense courage. Lieutenant Helmut Putz, aged only 24, was informed only a few hours beforehand that he had just 30 men to break into a building, where up to *seven* SS-men could be sleeping and put a noose around the Gauleiter's neck.[26]

Gerngross roamed restlessly through the countryside on his moped, ground down as much by excitement as exhaustion, and still unsure who he could truly depend upon when the crucial hour came. Reports that Giesler had declared a 'state of emergency' and hastily set up a court martial on April 11 just as their plans were being firmed up were worrying. Just as troubling was the sudden increase in the number of Gauleiter troops around the Central Ministry. "Something must have happened! Is there a Judas among the men?"

Brushing this dark thought aside, he told himself the die was already cast. It was not going to stop them now.[27]

Time seemed to stand agonisingly still. He prayed for his country's defeat, willing the US troops to draw closer. There would not be long to wait. On April 24, divisions from Patton's Seventh Army crossed the Danube and captured the city of Ulm, less than a hundred miles to the west. By April 26, they had reached the outskirts of Augsburg, less than fifty miles away, and Gerngross knew the time had finally come.

A few hours before addressing his men, he had turned on the radio to listen to the final episode of *Hagedorn*. Once again his words echoed. "The time has come for revolt against the Nazis," Hagedorn was telling his fighters. "Now is the time to strike! Down with the swastika, the symbol of death! Bring out the white flag of peace! Unconditional surrender to the Allies is Germany's only hope of salvation".[28]

Franz Ritter von Epp,
second from right standing next to Hitler. He betrayed
the FAB rebels at the last moment, saying he could
not bring himself to "abandon his friends. (Inset)
Former pub-bouncer, beer-hall thug and braggart, SS
Brigadier General Christian Weber. He was once
described as "the most despicable of Hitler's
underlings". When news broke of his capture, people
threw open their windows urging passing FAB troops
to 'Hang him, now!' Source: Bundesarchiv, Bild 119-
5590 / CC-BY-SA 3.0.

8

March had been unusually warm that year, but when April came, it grew steadily colder until the morning of the 27, when snow fell, covering the ground as Gerngross prepared to address the 180 men gathered in the barrack entrance hall. Some had already left for their mission. Others were learning for the first time what would be asked of them.

"Comrades, our task is to bring this senseless war to an end," he declared. "Hitler's 'Fortress Munich' cannot be allowed to happen. We must save what is left of our country from total destruction. That means taking action now. It means risking our lives.

"I call on you to follow me on the path to peace and freedom, but you must make the decision for yourselves. If any of you chooses not to join me, I will understand. But whoever follows me must be loyal to the end. As your commanding officer, I release you from your oath to Hitler. He has broken that oath to you many times over."[1]

Gerngross was all too well aware of the semi-mystical power the Führer still exerted over the men who served under him. The personal pledge of allegiance – obliging every German soldier to be prepared to lay down his life– was a key part of the personality cult the Nazi regime had built around its leader.

There could be no limits, no caveats, to the loyalty and obedience required for the triumph of the 'Thousand-year Reich'. So deeply was this embedded in the nation's consciousness that it was not unknown for soldiers, weeks after Hitler's suicide, to be heard wondering whether they were still actually bound by their pledge.[2] Gerngross felt that, only with a formal, ceremonial-like release in the presence of everyone could he cast out the demons, and lift the weight of obligation from his men's shoulders.

His fervour and passion sent an electric charge around the room and the answer was equally heartfelt: they ripped the Nazi insignia from their uniforms - some stamping on them or smearing them with the mud of their army boots. Strips of torn bedsheets were distributed as Gerngross explained that, under the rules of the Hague Land Warfare Convention, a white armband should signal to the enemy that they were no longer fighting members of the Wehrmacht.[3]

Some had brought strips of blue material to wear with the white, thus creating the Bavarian national colours as a personal 'battle standard'. To Gerngross' men this symbolised the new fight for their homeland's democratic values that had been crushed by the Nazis.

"It was strange,... intoxicating," one remembered vividly half a century later. "We had torn the NS insignia from our sleeves, we were leaping over a barrier we never thought we could cross, and at that moment, we were free as birds,"[4]

Gerngross had words of encouragement for all the men but singled out Eduard Schirovsky whose team was to seize control of the two Munich newspapers. It had not been an easy decision for the 41-year-old senior cadet officer to take part – his wife's uncle was the local NSDAP leader and a classic 'golden pheasant' - yet Schirovsky had swept aside any notion of divided loyalties and was seen by all the men as totally trustworthy.[5]

Finally, having armed themselves, his men gave the traditional, right-hand military salute, instead of the straight-arm, heel-clicking *Hitlergruß,* and went to work.

Oberleutnant (first lieutenant) Hans Betz and a troop of 45 hand-picked soldiers headed for the sprawling *Siedlung Sonnenwinkel* ('Sun Corner Settlement), a 'Nazi-Utopia' built in 1936 on 'blood and soil' principles idealising rural life, close to the town of Pullach seven miles away. He was to arrest, kidnap or kill General Siegfried Westphal, commander-in-chief of the *Wehrmacht* in the area, who was monitoring front line troop movements from its large communications centre , quartered in Hitler's personal 30-room wood-panelled bunker there.

Betz, 33, knew his mission would not be easy. He did not even have a plan of the bunker, but he was confident of taking the general by surprise. So confident, that he was already scheming to follow it up with a second operation the same night - capturing Munich's Lord Mayor Karl Fiehler, a notorious Nazi "yes-man", who often stayed overnight in the Rathaus *(City Hall)*.

Lieutenant Heuwing and a team of around 20 drove south to Lake Starnberg to cut phone and telegram links between Munich and Hitler's Berlin bunker by destroying the Nazi High Command communications centre at Kempfenhausen.

Another 65-strong unit headed into the city to seize control of the official Nazi Party newspapers, the *Völkischer Beobachter* and its smaller sister paper the *Münchner Neueste Nachrichten*. At the Munich *Reichsender* (Radio Munich, the main broadcasting station) just outside the town of Ismaning, north-east of the city, Braun's tanks were already in position, hidden behind bushes after rumbling out of the barracks at the dead of night on a "military exercise".Putz and his men had loaded three machine guns and several sackfuls of weapons into the back of an ambulance and left for the task of tracking down the Gauleiter[6] – others shouting after them to be sure to put a rope around his neck and hang the corpse from the ministry window for all to see.

With his men despatched, Gerngross stared impatiently at the phone. As if by order, it rang with the call he was waiting for, and with a handful of aides he hastened to the barrack gates, expecting to see the baker's van the unit had used to disguise their night-time reconnaissance trips. Instead, Gerngross found himself caught in the blinding headlights of a powerful

Mercedes driven by a Nazi-uniformed chauffeur.

Suddenly the chauffeur leaned forward, grinning at them from underneath an *Unteroffizier*'s (corporal's) peaked cap. It was Rödter: "We're taking over the city's newspapers, aren't we? Why not the car of the publisher, himself... I just, er, 'organised' it out of his garage."[7] Gerngross slumped with relief into the car belonging to millionaire publisher Max Amann. It had been 20 years since Amann had earned Hitler's favour by publishing his rambling autobiographical manifesto *Mein Kampf*, and had richly reaped the financial benefits.

Gerngross' heart was still pounding as they sped through the blacked-out, rainswept, streets. Betrayal at this crucial hour would have been catastrophic.

The heavy car pulled across the gravel in front of Reichstatthalter Epp's manor house headquarters on the shore of Lake Starnberg just after midnight. Seated in the back were Leiling, and, in his olive-green uniform, US airforce pilot Sid Leigh, who would 'witness' the uprising for the Allies. It was just after midnight and inside, Epp was holding an emergency meeting about food shortages with city officials.

Caracciola-Delbrück, looking agitated, ushered them into a library, lit by one small lamp, the black-out blinds pulled firmly down. Out of the hearing of the others, he whispered in exasperation: "Does it have to be now, Gerngross? Right at *this* very moment?" [8]

Gerngross was taken aback. "It's all arranged. We have done a deal with the enemy. There's no going back now." Caracciola-Delbrück looked alarmed. "Well, he's not in a good mood." Nonetheless he slipped into the neighbouring room leaving the door ajar and they saw him whisper in Epp's ear. The elderly General, in field uniform, rose stiffly to his feet and approached them, eyes narrowing. Caracciola-Delbrück introduced them and explained why they were there.

Epp's first response was incomprehension. Then, as what they were asking slowly dawned on him, he was appalled, but not for the reason they imagined. "I am a general, I cannot... place myself in the hands of a captain and...this... this American prisoner of war," he gestured at Leigh disdainfully. "It's impossible."[9]

This time it was Gerngross' and Leiling's turn to be appalled. They were mortified that, amid the apocalyptic reports of soldiers' deaths at the front, of there being only two days of food left in the city, the overriding concern of the man in whose hands the fate of Munich lay, was one of military protocol – they were too "lowly" in terms of rank for him to associate with them.

Time was running out. Was their rebellion so long in the planning now doomed? Exchanging glances but concealing their agitation, they calmly explained the plan again to the 76-year-old general. With Westphal kidnapped or killed and Giesler held by the FAB he, as governor, was the highest representative of the Reich in Bavaria. All he had to do was to announce by radio that he had assumed governmental powers and order German soldiers not to resist the Allied troops.

Gerngross gently reminded Epp that he, too, had, in 1919, led a coup d'etat against a regime he believed to be unjust. "General," he said, truthfully, "you are the only person we can turn to. We are unknown ... but you enjoy international respect. The Americans will trust your word. Lend our uprising your name, offer them the surrender of Bavaria and be Munich's saviour once more."

Caracciola-Delbrück went further: "General, you once told me yourself, in confidence, but perhaps I can break that confidence now, that, for a long time you have not felt able to support Hitler's policies. If you are prepared to stand up now, you can make good the injustices of those years."

"How long have you been planning this uprising?" Epp asked suspiciously. "Since 1933," Gerngross replied.[10] After a weary silence, Epp collapsed into a chair, his mouth twitching. "All the preparations for the defence of Munich are made. I can do nothing," he said with a wave of his hand. "Then," replied Gerngross sternly, "you are a prisoner of the Freedom Action of Bavaria."

"Where do you intend to take me?" Epp half-smiled. "To a broadcasting station to declare a state of emergency, call a ceasefire and surrender unconditionally to the Allies," replied Gerngross. "With you? Why, you are not even a staff officer," came the contemptuous observation.

Epp was tired and irritated; he had been just about to go to bed. He had distractedly left his gun on a table in the other room and Gerngross, Leiling and Leigh were armed with a submachine gun. He was furious that his guards were nowhere to be seen.

Stepping quietly forward, Leiling offered a solution: that the governor accompany them to Major Braun, where he would be dealing with someone of more "acceptable" rank.

"We'll go there immediately but I will travel in my own car," Epp declared.

Soon the convoy was speeding the forty miles to Freising, the large swastika pennant of his official car flapping in the streaming rain, triggering Hitler-salute reflexes from soldiers at checkpoints as they swept past.

Just before 2am, Gerngross and Leiling peeled off from the convoy, leaving Caracciola-Delbrück to ensure Epp was delivered to Braun, and hurried across town to join the men about to ambush Luftwaffe guards at the first, municipal radio station at Freimann. It was one regularly used to broadcast warnings of air-raids, and households stayed tuned in to it at night, listening out for the loud *"Achtung! Achtung!* that would catapult them from their warm beds into the cold damp of their cellars.

Breathless, as much with excitement as running, Gerngross and Leiling burst through the door of the radio station, only to find the reception area deserted. They stood momentarily bewildered, before recognising the voice of a FAB member on the station feed: *"Achtung! Achtung!..,"* he declared, deploying his linguist's skills to mimic the stentorian Nazi tones of the regular announcer. Then, after a pause: "This is the Freedom Action of Bavaria speaking. Codeword 'Pheasant Shoot'. *Repeat:* Pheasant Shoot is launched..."[11]

"The Freedom Action of Bavaria has this very night seized governmental power....and shaken off the Nazi yoke in Munich... Reich Governor Ritter von Epp is at the Freedom Action of Bavaria Combat Headquarters. ....Allied Forces are on our doorstep.... The FAB unites all opponents of National Socialism. Its goal is the complete elimination of National Socialism, the restoration of peace and democratic government and for the senseless fighting to end immediately.

"All opponents of National Socialism, who are of good will, are called on to take part together in the fight and play their part in the immediate end of the senseless fighting. Eliminate the officials of the National Socialist Party.....Deliver the death blow to the remaining Nazi overlords. *Achtung Achtung!*"

Slapping each other on the back, Gerngross and Leiling ran up the stairs and into the studio. Gerngross took over the microphone, recalling later how his heart was beating so loudly, he was convinced the microphone would pick it up. "This is the Freedom Action of Bavaria," he began, his voice wavering with nerves: "*Achtung! Achtung!* Stop the senseless murder. Lay down your arms – remove the Nazis wherever you find them.....Deliver the death-blow to the Nazi war-machine! Governor Epp is at the FAB command post. Hoist white flags, the Allied troops are approaching Munich!"[12]

Leiling was next. He directed his address to the

thousands of English and American PoWs living in desperate conditions, reassuring them in their own language that the FAB would restore human dignity. The same message was delivered in French, then Polish, Russian, Hungarian as the interpreters continued in a long list of tongues, creating waves of solidarity among internees and foreign slave labourers in the city's Nazi camps.

They could be reasonably certain their voices were being heard. For months, FAB sympathisers had been smuggling the parts of small, self-build radios into the camps.[13] They would spread the word among the 110,000 PoWs at Moosburg, the 5,000 Polish officers at *Oflag VII-A*, near the town of Murnau am Staffelsee, and 40 British officers imprisoned at *Stalag 383/Z*, at Steinburg, near Straubing.

Within an hour, a messenger appeared with the news that a FAB unit had overpowered the 40 armed SS guards at the second radio station at Ismaning and were now running Munich Reich Broadcasting. After overcoming their initial astonishment at being attacked by soldiers from their own side, the staff had refused Nazi station manager Alois Wolf's calls to immediately sabotage the equipment, and he was dragged from the newsroom wailing abjectly: "*Mein Führer, mein Führer*, how you have been betrayed!"[14]

Gerngross' insistence on hiring radio specialists had paid off for the FAB. They only discovered on arrival at the station that it had no microphones. Everything was set up simply to relay pre-prepared programmes. A makeshift apparatus was quickly assembled allowing Gerngross to announce at 7am: "The pheasant shoot is underway."

Soon the word was spreading across Munich, with Nazi officials waking, amid fury and confusion, to hear police, civil servants, public transport workers and employees of water and electricity works being urged to defy Hitler's 'Nero' instructions and save the city from destruction.

Messengers on mopeds were criss-crossing the city, bringing Gerngross encouraging news of vigilante groups being formed to arrest local Nazi leaders. DOLKO member and Olympic athlete Nieberl was illegally cycling down the motorway at breakneck speed bringing in further reports of FAB rebellions from far-flung villages. All this was being broadcast live, further fuelling the uprising.[15]

Other reports spoke of the German front line crumbling in disarray with as many as 20,000 soldiers laying down their weapons and deserting. FAB operatives under Heuwing were interrupting military communications, sewing more confusion. [16] Luftwaffe soldiers had started destroying their own airbase at nearby *Schleißheim*.[17]

Not everything had gone smoothly. At the start of their attack on General Westphal's bunker, Betz and his men had been heavily set upon by a special SS-unit drafted in at the last minute. Unable to reach the general, they had imprisoned him and his staff by blowing up all the exits of the deep bunker in which he had made his headquarters. He was held captive by the blocked exits for two days, managing to clear a way out only hours before the arrival of the American troops.[18] Betz had gone on to unexpectedly bag a far greater "golden pheasant", one of the fattest of the flock: the odious former Beer-Hall thug turned SS Brigadier, Christian Weber.[19]

Weber had decided to spend the night in his office in the *Marienplatz* City Hall and was still holed up there when Betz and his men stumbled upon him. Rejecting his craven attempt to buy freedom with 5,000 Reichsmark cheque, they threw the SS Brigadier General into the back of a lorry.[20] News of this prize capture delighted the FAB's growing radio audience, and the men in white armbands found themselves being cheered from open windows to loud cries of "Hang him, now!" [21]

Munich's police headquarters were in the hands of the FAB. Factory workers with arms supplied by FAB members mounted roadblocks to keep out SS units, and derail trains they suspected of carrying Nazi reinforcements. Workers at three of the region's largest armaments factories - the Agfa Werk, the BMW factory and the Steinheil optical company - downed tools and kept guard over their worksites with weapons supplied by the FAB to prevent the Nazis from destroying them.

Explosives placed by Nazi loyalists, and primed to destroy the city's main bridges were found and removed. Electricity and water supplies were secured. Across the region, barricades and trenches put in place to halt the expected Allied tank advance were being swept aside or filled in.[22]

A sea of fluttering white flags, crowned by a particularly majestic one, made from three large bedsheets, draped from the tower of the city's historic *Frauenkirche* church, would now guide the US Army in. The giant swastika that flew from the City Hall had been replaced with a blue and white Bavarian flag.[23]

Ernst Baur, a 26-year-old assistant doctor, described the "sheer joy" of seeing so many white flags as he cycled through the ruined streets of the city that morning. "Everywhere there were white bedsheets hanging from windows.... ordinary people were demonstrating courageously, clearly and openly, that they had had enough of the megalomania, the obsessive destruction and the fakery of the psychopath in the Reich Chancellery bunker. The spectre of a thousand-year tyranny had been banished"[24]

A new newspaper called *Bayerische Nachrichten* ("Bavarian News") was being laid out and would soon be rolling off the printing presses to record the night's events.

Messages poured in from German exiles to say the FAB's voice was now being heard across Europe - from Italy, where fighting was still going on, to Norway. Radio Luxemburg and the BBC in London had picked up the FAB broadcasts and started to relay them around the world.[25]

They were also being heard by General Patton's Third Army sweeping victoriously down to Munich from Nuremberg, his Sherman tanks thundering along Hitler's *Autobahn* (motorway), once the pride of Nazi Germany.[26]

The FAB's fears that the Nazis would mobilise their 60,000-strong *Volkssturm* (People's Militia) troops, against them quickly faded. [27] Hitler's Munich 'Nero' plan had assumed that this 'Dad's Army' of men too old, young, or unfit to fight would rally to the cause. Battalion by battalion, they were, instead, throwing their weapons into the River Isar and going home. [28]

At local level the Nazis had, in fact, shown a humiliating lack of resolve. Porcelain factory manager Karl Wieninger, a FAB supporter, who later became a German MP, remembered bursting armed through the front door of his local Nazi *Bonze* ('fat cat'), to see his deputy *Ortsgruppenleiter* (group leader) "dressed only in his underpants, weeping at his kitchen table and clinging to his weapons because he was afraid of being shot by the Americans." [29]

The radio broadcasts saved the lives of many of the 7,000 Jews, already emaciated and disease-ridden, being forced on a *Todesmarsch* from Dachau concentration camp to the Austrian border in driving snow. The SS guards, driving them on with whips and shooting those too weak to walk, were thrown into confusion by the reports coming over the airwaves. They "lost their nerve, threw away their weapons and, more or less, let these concentration camp prisoners run away and in this way they regained their freedom," Gerngross recalled. "Some of the things we heard about astonished us." [30]

Also protected were the lives of around 40 British officers facing a similar march from their PoW camp *Stalag 383/Z*, at Steinburg Castle, near Straubing.

Their camp commander Ernst Falkner, an early FAB member, defied orders and made sure the PoWs stayed put.[31]

Like a fuse being lit, the radio broadcasts sparked a trail of rebellion that raced around the city and deep into the countryside. To many, waking up that morning to hear voices calling for peace and democracy, it was clear something momentous had happened: thousands answered the call. Rumours even began to circulate that Hitler was already dead.

Fears that the Allies might not keep their promise to call off bombing raids quickly evaporated. Later it would be revealed that a gigantic massive arsenal had been set aside for the obliteration of the city - a total of 2,400 bombs, one for every 200 people.[32] But that night the uprising took place under silent skies.

FAB members were elated. Everything seemed to have gone "like clockwork", Gerngross recalled. Around 600 SS men had been sleeping in the Freimann barracks less than half a mile from the first radio station, yet the FAB were able to broadcast for a total of almost twelve hours with no interference from the "terror-robots". There had been no sign, either, of Hitler's secret Nazi guerrillas, the Werewolves. "That we were not disturbed until 7am, despite being right nextdoor to SS barracks (two kilometres!) is pretty much astounding."[33]

Exhausted but jubilant, Gerngross and his men toasted their "peaceful revolution". They consoled themselves that work – begun in the ashes of the Valkyrie plot – proved that Stauffenberg and his associates had not died in vain. Well-wishers at the city's renowned *Riemersch Likörfabrik* distillery had smuggled a case of cognac to the FAB fighters "to calm everyone's nerves". Every soldier had filled a flask and now thankfully drained it.[34]

In the early hours of April 28, reports of the uprising reached Hitler's Berlin bunker. According to a diary entry for 00.30am at the *Oberkommando der Wehrmacht* (OKW – Armed Forces High Command), Colonel General Alfred Jodl, Army Chief of Operations Staff, demanded the "calls to mutiny by a 'Bavarian Freedom Committee' being broadcast over the airwaves from the Munich Radio station be stopped immediately."[35]

When they learned that Reichsleiter Martin Bormann had telegraphed Giesler ordering him to: "Defend your district with unyielding harshness," they all laughed uproariously. "It met with derision," wrote Gerngross. "Too late now!"[36] The FAB even took to ridiculing the Gauleiter openly over the airwaves: "Paul Giesler, where are you?" they asked mockingly.[37]

But the question was more pressing than Gerngross would admit. Far from having a noose around his neck, Giesler was not only alive and well but seemed to have been expecting them that night. His guards had lain in wait for Putz and his men and ambushed them when they came within inches of the building – hurling a barrage of grenades from the upper floor windows. The FAB men had been forced to retreat, injured and empty-handed.[38]

The news sent a shiver of fear and disbelief around

the rebels at the radio station newsroom. The street around the Gauleiter's bunker had been checked less than three hours before the uprising began, noting only a few extra soldiers on guard. But by the time Putz and his men arrived, just a few hours later, fresh *Volkssturm* troops had moved in to surround the building housing Giesler's bunker. They had even got cannons out!

There *must* be a spy in the camp! "Even close to home, there was a traitor," Gerngross realised. "I am sure it was someone in the company because Giesler's guards were ready to fight to defend him... they had even, as I learned later, rolled a cannon out onto the street.[39]..... We had had fleeting suspicions about a certain soldier. We can't, of course, prove it..... [but]...we knew it would only work if it was carried out in the form of a 'surprise' raid. It [our raid] didn't succeed because *in some way* they were prepared for us."[40]

Giesler's spies had, in fact, been busy that night - all had not gone well for Schirovsky's newspaper team, either. When they pulled up outside the printing presses and editorial offices of the *Völkischen Beobachters* in the *Schellingstrasse* shortly after 1am, there was no sign of 32-year-old Sergeant Erich Fendl, who had offered machine-gun cover as they seized control of the newspaper. When they stormed the main entrance with the few men and arms they had, two shadowy figures fled into the interior of the building slamming doors shut behind them.

Fearing the staff had been secretly tipped off and

his men were about to come under attack, Schirovsky retreated and switched to the offices and printing presses of the smaller *Münchner Neueste Nachrichten* newspaper a short distance away[41], which they seized without problems.

Their suspicions deepened when, just as they were hard at work producing the newspaper and FAB leaflets, two lorries driven by soldiers pulled up unexpectedly outside purportedly with orders from Gerngross to take them to the Radio Munich station, where the SS were closing in.

Not only did the soldiers not know the secret FAB password but they had instructions, unusually, written on a piece of paper. Believing it to be a genuine 'SOS' some men immediately jumped aboard the lorry. But Schirovsky did not believe Gerngross would fail to observe his own 'never-write-anything-down' rule at this critical moment and suspected it was a trap set by the SS. He ordered the drivers to head, instead, for the secret underground railway passage, the FAB's rebellion headquarters, where he could verify the orders. He would lead the way in his car, keeping close tabs on the trucks behind him.

He sprang into the vehicle, only to find it mysteriously would not start and was left furious but helpless as the lorries drove off without him.

"At the break of dawn, a Luftwaffe officer and his team arrived in a lorry and ordered everyone to 'jump in'. Quite a few obeyed and ended up in the hands of those determined to drag out the war," he recalled later.[42]

Schirovsky was *sure* he knew who had betrayed them. "It occurred to me that as we were leaving the barracks, Sergeant Erich Fendl, who was armed with a submachine gun (which we didn't have), wanted to join in with my team of 65 men. Then suddenly he disappeared. We didn't trust him because the boss (Gerngross) had already had to discipline him once. We suspected betrayal which we believed was confirmed by what happened at the *Völkischer Beobachter*." He believed Fendl had not known about the switch to the second newspaper, but sent the lorries once he found out.[43]

This was all deeply troubling for Gerngross. Perhaps they had been betrayed by a whole *nest* of spies. His suspicions fell on a man keen to join them, thought to have offered technical radio skills. He pulled out - but not before he had "completely failed us at the last moment."[44]

Was this why they had been unable to capture Reich Defence Commissar Giesler, a key component of their plan to prevent the Nazis destroying Munich – or General Westphal? The Dachau death march had begun just a day before the uprising? Had the SS known of the FAB's plans to prevent it? And where was Epp? He and Braun should have been at the radio station *hours* ago. And by all calculations, the American troops should have crossed the Danube and entered the city by now. Where were they and where, now, was Giesler?

Munich's Lord Mayor Karl Fiehler (centre, behind Chamberlain in 1938), an anti-semite, who took to the airwaves with Giesler to try to bring Munich back under Nazi control and to demonstrate that he had not been captured by FAB rebels. (inset) Gauleiter Paul Giesler, whose loyalty to Hitler was 'ferocious'. He ordered the execution of the White Rose resistance movement and vowed to hunt down and 'liquidate' every member of the FAB. He planned to poison or shoot the 25,000 concentration camp prisoners as the US troops approached. Hitler was to reward his fanaticism by naming him Reich Minister for the Interior in his will of 29 April 1945.

9

Giesler was, in fact, settling down in front of a microphone himself, and was about to broadcast an address on the very frequency the FAB had used a few hours earlier. He was enraged and humiliated to have come under attack the previous night - not from enemy forces - but from a handful of rebels within his own Reich army. He was about to tell listeners that what had happened during the night was "a ghastly business" but it would soon be over. It would, but not in the way he imagined.[1]

He had always been fervently proud that Hitler had placed Munich, the city he saw as a bastion of loyalty, in *his* hands when he appointed him as Gauleiter. Accordingly, he ruled it as he thought the Führer would have done - with ruthlessness and zero tolerance for dissent.

The suggestion that he had lost control of the city to a rag-tag bunch of rebels filled him with fury. The FAB spies in the ministry had not been exaggerating when they reported Giesler to have stormed around the ministry in an "apocalyptic" rage when it came under attack. [2]

There was another pressing matter on his mind that cold April morning. Hitler, he knew, was drafting his last 'political will and testament', which would almost certainly elevate Giesler to the post of Interior Minister - one of the highest positions in the post-Hitler government.[3] This was a job Giesler had long coveted – one that would bestow on him the same status and privileges enjoyed by members of the Führer's inner circle, which included both Himmler and Bormann.

He was not going to have this long-awaited prize and the "reward" Hitler wished to give him after years of faithful service, snatched out of his hands by an unknown, junior-ranking 'traitor'. No, the rebellion would be crushed, every member hunted down and, in the insensate Nazi euphemism he liked to use, "liquidated".

It was 9.56am when Giesler began broadcasting a hastily put-together statement. Mocking Gerngross' name by calling him *"Gernegross"* (*gerne* means 'would like' and *gross* means 'great'), he thundered: "A bunch of dishonest comrades from an interpreting company, led by a would-be big noise, are trying to give the impression they have taken power in Munich, using the names of higher-ranking officers. No-one will follow a *'Gernegross'*, who is selling out Germany. He will not escape his punishment." [4]

The intention was for every FAB member to clearly understand that nothing less than execution – both for them and their families – would be the price of treachery. Once found and dragged from their hiding places they could expect the usual welcome at Gestapo HQ in *Prinz Albrechtstraße*. What happened next came as a shock.

Far from being cowed into silence, FAB voices were immediately heard again on the avowedly-secure Reichsender frequency. Their message was to ignore the toadying Gauleiter, that the respected figure of Epp was now calling for an end to the "senseless fighting" and talking of "the new leadership" under which the "bloodshed will not continue nor the tragedy..... of Germans fighting Germans.." 5

Driven to new heights of rage, Giesler, ordered the closest Luftwaffe base, *Luftflotte 6* in *Oberföhring*, five miles away, to bomb the rebel-held radio station and destroy its transmitter. When the reply came back that the few planes available were grounded by bad weather, 300 soldiers were ordered to march to the station and cut the transmission cable.6

He then summoned Karl Fiehler to help him reinforce Nazi authority over the city. The 49-year-old Lord Mayor had spent the morning listening to official broadcast reports of his death. In the confusion that was slowly consuming the city, a report had gone out that he had been captured and killed by the rebels, as they had planned.

Now, as Giesler and an emphatically alive Fiehler prepared their speeches, an announcer came on, urging listeners to 'stand by their radio sets'. 7

At 12.30pm, just as most families were sitting down to lunch, the station's dance melodies were interrupted by the announcer reassuring them that the "criminal elements under the so-called leadership of a Captain *Gernegross* have been neutralised. All authorities, officials and posts in the entire southern area of our Greater German Fatherland are, of course, firmly in the control of those unconditionally loyal to the Reich and the Führer."

The "treasonous shirkers" would have "immediate and merciless measures" taken against them, he declared. "*All* of their claims of success were, naturally, fictitious." These people were no more than "miserable wretches," he went on,who had "needed to steal the names of leaders of the National Socialist movement and our army."

Then came Giesler's clipped and precise tones: "At about 2am, a brigade of shirkers, who unfortunately call themselves soldiers, but belong to a company of interpreters and have never smelt powder in this war, tried to overthrow my authority using two machine guns. My *Volkssturmers* threw a hand grenade, and they fled, leaving their weapons behind...

"Do not take their claims seriously. Not a word of it is true," he thundered. This scum, which is trying to incite you, these bedsit revolutionaries, only want to plunder and set up mob rule. We will cut them to pieces in a space of a few hours. These disreputable scoundrels, who want to defile the name of Germany in this darkest hour will soon be shot and snuffed out."

The address built to a rousing peroration: "The people of Munich will never turn against the brave soldiers, who are fighting the enemy," cried Giesler.

"The people of Munich will always think of the dead they have lost and will never be drawn away from their loyalty to Germany and to Adolf Hitler. In this loyalty and this love, we abide. Long live Germany. Long live the Führer! Heil Hitler!"

Fiehler, still furious over reports of his death, wanted a final word. "This traitorous group of shirkers have today again stated that I am dead. The fact that I am now speaking to you will prove... that these rogues are nothing but vile swindlers.

"All honest men can feel nothing but disgust at these frauds... do not think that people who get into bed with our enemies have the welfare of the people of Munich in mind. They don't want to help you or us, only exploit and destroy our people by aiding and abetting our enemies...We, the Munich people, are with the Führer, with all our hearts. He is in Berlin, directing the final battle. Heil to our Führer!"

Listeners were so captivated by the drama being played out on their *Volksempfänger* that Saturday morning, many could not bear to break off to go out. One described it as "a wild war of the airwaves".[8]

Who was telling the truth? At the neutral Swiss Consulate in the nearby town of *Rottach-Egern*, staff monitoring the broadcasts noted: "The freedom movement is stronger than supposed, and in control of almost the entire city. Every shot is downing a golden pheasant! Nazi big-wigs are said to be hanging from trees."

At Munich Reich broadcasting, the rebels had just taken a short break from announcements when an alarm sounded. Giesler's men had reached the power station at *Finsing*, located the cable that supplied the transmitter and cut it. The music stopped abruptly followed by silence.⁹

Large deployments of SS troops were now moving across the city. Realising they were outgunned and outnumbered, the FAB leaders overruled those who wanted to stay and fight on. The only sensible course was strategic retreat. The men, still in high spirits, agreed to disperse. "After... the call to stop this senseless war had been broadcast repeatedly, and with several SS units closing in... our job looked to be done," one wrote later.¹⁰ Clearly, they could have had no idea of what was to come.

In small groups, they vanished, some into the forests north of Freising, others slipping into the dense mist blanketing the Erding wetlands, burying the tell-tale records of their DOLKO membership in the marshes It was not a moment too soon. Barely had they left the station, than the heavily armed SS-Division *Nordach,* arrived from their barracks.

Realising that his window of opportunity was closing, Grengross set off on a desperate mission to finally secure Epp's support.

When the Reich governor's official car had pulled into the gravel driveway of Braun's Haidberghof manor house at *Pettenbrunn* the night before, Epp had expected to speak with Braun alone. Instead, he was led into a large room, to be confronted by eight officers, each clutching detailed reports about the desperate state of affairs at the front.

Epp hid his irritation and dutifully listened to them, but he was tired and disorientated. His mood appeared to swing from polite distrust to genuine concern. As the officers outlined their troops' plight, he sat, nervously turning his inlaid cigarette case over and over in his hand, then - as one present described it - suddenly "lifting both hands in despair, as if the apocalyptic scenes they painted of Germany's finest soldiers being cut to pieces were passing before his eyes, he cried out: "No, no... they are still out there fighting...." [11]

Just at that moment, through an open door, Epp caught his name being broadcast, along with a FAB call to hunt down the 'golden pheasants' and "defeat militarism". He stared down at the gold party badge on his chest. He had fought in two world wars, militarism had been the core of his life. Then a spirit of defiance began to stir in him. "Gentlemen," he announced, "for as long as German soldiers are fighting, and while I have friends in the party, I cannot stab them in the back." [12]

Caracciola-Delbrück took Epp to a side room, where he immediately slumped onto a sofa and slept for 20 minutes. When he awoke, the two men spent a tortuous further *four hours* in deep discussion and still Epp could not be convinced that he should lend the FAB rebellion his name and negotiate a peaceful surrender with the Allies.

The next day, Gerngross, riding pillion on a messenger's motorbike almost, literally, ran into Braun, who was likewise trying to find Gerngross.

Braun could only deliver the depressing news that Epp had refused to abandon his 'friends' (the Nazis). "I had to let the old fool go home," Braun reported despairingly.[13]

But Epp had not gone home. Ernst Röhm had once been his chief of staff and he knew only too well what could happen if you dared to rise up against Hitler. Epp had gone straight to report the matter to Nazi High Command at Kempfenhausen, mentally drafting the report he anticipated being asked to compile for Hitler. Instead, he was arrested.

Caracciola-Delbrück, ever the loyal aide, resolved to share the fate of the man he had followed faithfully for so many years. Epp had always protected him and he was determined he would not abandon the general at this moment.

But on arrival in Giesler's bunker, they were separated.The interrogators concentrated their efforts on Caracciola-Delbrück while a relieved Epp, was spared "harsher measures" due to his "advanced age".[14] He later claimed that no one ever mentioned what became of his loyal aide.[15]

Gerngross said Caracciola-Delbrück simply "could not bring himself to step aside", but instead accompanied Epp "out of vassal-like allegiance, seeing death before his eyes."[16]

Later that day, Gerngross' parents, who had been brought into the Central Ministry by one of Giesler's snatch squads, were shocked to see Caracciola-Delbrück appear to them "like a ghost" in torn uniform, his face "bearing the signs of torture" as he

was led at gunpoint by a drunken guard to his
execution in the ministry courtyard. He loyally refused
until the last to reveal details of his fellow FAB
members' whereabouts, saying repeatedly: "I do not
understand....". He was despatched by pistol with a
bullet to the head.[17]

Priest Josef Grimm (left), who pulled down the large swastika flag that flew from the village church tower. He was taken away by the SS for interrogation. The next day his parishioners found his corpse dumped in a roadside grave. He was still clutching a rosary in his left hand. Picture courtesy of the private archive of Dr Helmut Moll, Cologne, author of: "Zeugen für Christus – Das Deutsche Martyrologium des 20. Jahrhunderts". (Right) SA Brigadeführer Hans Zöberlein. The 100-strong 'Werewolf commando' he led was responsible for the Penzberg massacre in which sixteen resistance fighters were shot or hanged. Together with Giesler and Hübner, he made up what Gergross called the "killing-troika".

10

There was no doubt in Giesler's mind that Hitler's 'Alpine Fortress' existed. His bags were already packed, but before he left the "ghastly business" in Munich to begin a new life there, he would take the lives of those determined to bring down what was left of the Führer's once-glorious Reich.

Time was short and, with American troops almost at the gates of the city, he summoned help from two men he knew he could rely on – Captain Alfred Salisco, the irascible commander of an elite, "special deployment" *Volkssturm* batallion and SA Brigade Leader Hans Zöberlein, one of Hitler's 'old fighters', who controlled the shadowy elite Werewolf squads taken from Hitler Youth camps and trained for covert military tactics.

Additional help was on the way from Lieutenant General Rudolf Hübner, a man Hitler, himself, was said to have described as a "fanatical and reliable Nazi".

Hübner had been among the Wehrmacht forces being pushed southwards as the Allies advanced. When he heard the audacious FAB radio broadcasts, he remained calm, confident Giesler could use the special court martial powers Hitler had personally bestowed upon him. Hübner had no legal experience but Hitler conferred the powers, knowing he could count on him to take revenge on the five German officers who failed to blow up the Remagen bridge. By the end of the war, the 'flying court martial', originally set up to hear urgent charges of offences committed in the field, had become little more than a kangaroo court designed to have people sentenced to death within minutes. There was no appeal.

On arrival in the city, Hübner strode purposefully through the arched entrance of the Central Ministry and offered his services. Giesler was inclined to accept, but first made discreet checks on Hübner's personal military file. There he found a cautionary note dated March 15 1945: "Unquestioning, fervent National Socialist... in his zeal for tasks he sometimes goes too far and needs controlling".[1] It was *precisely* what Giesler was looking for.

After a quick phone-call seeking the permission of General Field Marshal Albert Kesselring, Giesler returned. He shook Hübner's hand heartily and appointed him Munich's 'Combat Commander'.

In extraordinary scenes, an estimated 150 people were sentenced to death that day by the three Nazis, who made up what Gerngross called Giesler's "killing-troika", revelling in what the FAB leader describes as "an ecstasy of hate-filled revenge".[2] A "great pool of blood" spread over the ministry courtyard as suspects, often with no connection to the FAB, were taken out and killed.3 The bunker, itself, was the size of a small bus depot but, as the backlog of executions mounted, its corridors grew crowded and guards were forced to load prisoners onto lorries and execute them in the nearby Perlach Forest, tied to trees.

Such profuse vengefulness bore all the hallmarks of the senseless, cold-blooded Nazi violence cloaked in the small print of legal order and officialdom that would continue until the last minute of the regime's existence.

Amid the bloodshed and the drunkenness - *Volkssturmers* were routinely plied with alcohol as they queued to carry out the killing orders - death sentences were carefully written out by hand, forms duly filled in and rubber stamped, distance rules strictly paced out by firing squads according to military guidelines. One witness described seeing "a pile of forms lying on a desk" when he visited the bunker in the afternoon of April 28. "Someone told me he would have to take the pile across (the bunker) because the 150 people (concerned) still had to be liquidated, they (the forms) were the death sentences of the flying court martial."4

The veneer of process was cast off as soon as the corpses were taken out of the building covered in tarpaulins. Some were buried in shallow graves, others dumped in bomb craters. An entry in the war diary of the Wehrmacht High Command for April 29 states approvingly that: "of the Munich mutineers, 200 people had been either shot or hanged".5

While Hübner had those brought to him in

Giesler's bunker interrogated and sentenced, Zöberlein and a 200-strong Werewolf squad fanned out into the countryside with orders to 'deal' with the 'politically unreliable' on the spot. He barely knew where to start - fresh prey was breaking cover in all directions. It would be easy prey, too: few ordinary Germans in the villages carried guns. "Zöberlein simply went to the places where it would be easiest for him, where he would not come across people, who were armed, and killed them. It was an utterly shameful operation," recalled Gerngross.[6]

Few of those earmarked for death had time to flee or even hide before the SS troops stormed their villages. One man, who happened to be driving along the riverbank between *Dirnismaning* and *Freimann* that Saturday morning suddenly came across SS-men marching armed with submachine guns and barely able to walk for the weight of bullets in their belts. "I knew what they (the bullets) were for," he observed bitterly.[7]

It was in small, close-knit, often religious communities that Gerngross's message resonated most powerfully. But the people living in them were no match for the Nazi Werewolves, whose reputation for savagery was well-deserved.

A leaflet picturing their "Wolf's hook" was distributed in the *Sendling* district of Munich. The mythical device, a crescent shaped piece of iron with a chain baited with meat, was believed to have magical powers and was hung from trees to trap wolves in medieval times. It was an early Nazi party symbol and used by many German divisions, including the Waffen-SS. The leaflet read: "Warning to all traitors and harlots of the enemy! The Werewolf of Upper Bavaria is warning all those who aid and abet the enemy and any Germans or their relatives, who threaten or bully those who hold to their faith in Adolf Hitler. Traitors and criminals will forfeit their lives and the lives of their entire clan.

"Villages that sin against the life of our people or show the white flag will sooner or later suffer *Charivari*. Our revenge is fatal!" It is signed: "The Werewolf of Upper Bavaria". [8]

The terror the leaflets generated in ordinary villagers made flushing out the rebels an easy task for Zöberlein's men. Bewildered families, whose hope, a few hours earlier, had been to save themselves from the bombs and bullets of the Allies, were now frantically trying to fend off assaults from fellow Germans. In their desire to protect their loved ones, some cracked and revealed names.

One of the most notorious attacks happened in *Penzberg*, where a group of townspeople attempted to take over their local coalmine to prevent the Nazis from blowing it up. Enraged at this defiance of Hitler's 'Nero' plan, an officer from the local Wehrmacht unit, rounded up the ringleaders and had them arrested. He then drove the 34 miles to Munich to inform Giesler personally of this outrage and was told the eight men were to be shot immediately, without trial. They were executed on his return at 6pm in a copse overlooking the colliery.

That evening, fearing that the job might have been left unfinished, Giesler sent Zöberlein and a 100-strong Werewolf squad to the town. The SA brigade leader demanded to know *more* names of resistance fighters and was given eight, including those of two women, one pregnant. As soon as they were brought out, a placard was placed around their necks with the word: "Werewolf" on it and all but two men, who escaped, were hanged at various points around the town as a warning. The very next day, the American troops arrived.[9]

Most terrifying were the 'invisible' Werewolves, who left their signature warnings on the corpses of their murder victims before vanishing like ghosts. In *Mering*, 30 miles north-west of Munich, trader Andreas Wunsch had been hunted down and captured by the local *Volkssturm* after he stood outside the town hall on the morning of Saturday April 28, spreading word of the FAB's rebellion.

Augsburg's police president had him taken by car to a flying court martial. Six days later his corpse was found three miles from the town, riddled with machine gun bullets. A note found in his pocket read: "Anyone who is unfaithful to his people will be crushed by us Werewolves!!!"

The emergence of the Werewolves was not the only tragic unintended consequence of the FAB's call to arms that night. Diehard Nazis also rose up in unforeseen ways, eager to demonstrate their individual, last-gasp loyalty to Hitler.

In *Altötting*, one of Germany's most visited

Catholic shrines, word had spread that council leader Josef Kehrer had detained six local NSDAP officials in the local police cells. It reached the ears of a highly-decorated Lieutenant Colonel Karl Kaehne, who was undergoing treatment for hepatitis in a nearby military hospital. So incensed was Kaehne, 46, that he dragged himself from his sickbed and headed to *Altötting*, where he demanded to speak to Kehrer alone. He then shot Kehrer in the head, released the Nazi prisoners and promptly returned to his hospital bed. [10]

It took very little to provoke such extreme Nazi loyalists. Priest Josef Grimm had hauled down the large swastika that flew, by government decree, from his church tower in the village of Götting and replaced it with the Bavarian standard. Noticing the swap, a local Wehrmacht officer forced him at gunpoint to retrieve the Nazi flag from a gutter and hoist it again.

This wasn't the end of the matter. SS men arrived and took the priest away to be given over to the *Sicherheitsdienst* (Nazi Security Service). The next day his corpse, displaying signs of torture, was discovered dumped in a shallow roadside grave covered with pine branches. He was still clutching a rosary in his left hand.[11]

But, despite the savagery, some villagers stood up to the Nazis with remarkable acts of defiance. Less than 36 hours after the murder of their council leader, families in *Altötting* heard US troops urging them, in loudspeaker announcements from the opposite bank of the River Inn, to signal they were prepared to surrender by leaving their house lights on all night. To thwart any cooperation, the town's Nazi leader ordered the local electricity station to be shut down. When protesters gathered at its gates to prevent soldiers from entering, SS men fired into the crowd killing 41-year-old electrician Max Storfinger.

Still the townspeople continued to defy their Nazi masters. Candles were secretly handed to every family by a local shopkeeper and, as darkness fell, they lined the riverbank holding hands and clutching a lit candle desperately hoping the US troops on the other side would see them. They did, but fierce resistance by heavily-armed Nazi loyalists still prevented them from entering the town for a further four days.[12]

There was success, too, for the FAB at Dachau, where the broadcasts may have helped to save the lives of the remaining camp prisoners by inspiring two rebel groups to take action. Helped by former inmates, smuggled out and hidden in a barn, they seized the town hall and stripped local Hitler Youth of the weapons they had been given to defend the town. When Nazi leaders ordered their *Volkssturm* troops to attack, the soldiers instead switched sides and joined in the uprising.

The revolt proved no match for a still heavily-armed local SS Panzer division, who crushed it in a matter of hours, leaving the corpses of seven insurgents in the street as a 'warning'. But it is thought to have saved the town from destruction and prompted many of the SS concentration camp administrators to flee. A secretly formed International

Prisoners Committee was then able to persuade the few remaining SS men to halt the planned murder or death march of any further prisoners.

The following morning, the camp was liberated.

There were narrow escapes. In *Penzberg* one man managed to get away when the rope around his neck snapped, and he fled in a hail of bullets. A pub landlord from the Westend district of Munich refused to climb onto one of his own barrels to be hung and argued so vociferously that he had been falsely accused, the execution squad released him.

Giesler, appalled to learn that a man entrusted with an entire tank unit had betrayed him, despatched several buses full of armed military police to Major Braun's Freising barracks with orders to bring him and his men back "dead or alive" but they were already in hiding and could not be found.

Gerngross' parents were interrogated but wisely maintained they had broken off contact with their son because of 'political differences'. Giesler kept them alive, confident they would eventually reveal Gerngross' whereabouts but, having ordered Munich's workforce to stay at their posts, he fled the approaching US Army. Although he was still issuing death sentences as his car and motorcade were revving up ready for his departure, theirs was not among them and they were set free.[13]

Gerngross' return to the Radio Munich station had been delayed by having to divert to avoid SS-units now scattered across the city. He arrived just as the last men were leaving, then drove north to *Landshut* to find the US Army. If he had misjudged the timing of its troops' arrival in Munich, he desperately needed to find the Americans now – and fast.

By late afternoon, exhausted, he fell asleep at the wheel and ploughed his car into a ditch close to a military hospital. Standing outside it was a tall German medical officer wearing an old "Blücher" army field cap, a coded signal of old-fashioned military honour. When Gerngross introduced himself, the officer, recognising the name, took a step forward and stretched out his hand warmly, saying: "Respect, Captain". He arranged for Gerngross to stay overnight at his son's farmhouse in the nearby village of *Binsham*. They would provide him with a Bavarian hunter's *Lederhosen* and braces disguise.[14]

Relieved, Gerngross hastened to the farm, where he gratefully ditched his uniform and fell asleep that night listening to the drone and gabble of drunken voices from a barn full of sheltering Wehrmacht deserters outside his window.

He was jolted awake at dawn by a deafening roar from the skies and rumble and clatter on all sides. Throwing back the farmhouse shutters, a glorious sight greeted him: fleets of Sherman tanks were churning through the mud on either side of the farmhouse, American. fighter bombers thundered in the skies above them while, in the distance, columns of American. soldiers, many men deep, were marching in untidy formations towards him as far as the eye could see.

"As the early morning mist cleared, I could see the

giant war-machine of a US division spread across the entire valley. There were soldiers arriving in squad columns, marching on both sides of the street. The Americans were in possession of all the land in and around *Landshut*." [15]

The journalist and broadcaster
Noel Newsome who met
Gerngross as the Americans
arrived – among them the
future novelist J. D. Salinger
(right).

11

The mysterious night-time exhortations to rise up against the Nazi regime from inside Germany stirred great interest among the international press corps. American reporter Joel Sayre, who was in Munich, filed a powerful despatch to the *New Yorker* magazine describing his astonishment at finding himself "reporting the fairly incredible fact that somewhere in Germany I saw living Germans, who had risked their lives fighting the Nazis."[1]

Among those whose imagination it also fired was a war correspondent working for the newly-liberated Radio Luxemburg. Noel Newsome had been director of European broadcasts for the BBC, but was now on secondment to Radio Luxembourg as the voice of Eisenhower's headquarters, SHAEF. He had already been told by the new BBC director-general, William Haley, that he was he was "too much of a crusader" to continue in his job – a judgement he took pride in, and promptly ignored.[2]

On the night of April 27 1945, he was broadcasting from the newly-liberated Radio Luxembourg station, knowing his reports would be picked up by the BBC

Monitoring Service. Determined to be one of the first to interview the man whose "anti-Nazi organisation ....was fighting the SS in the streets of the city", he set off the next morning to enter Munich with the American troops, find Gerngross and tell his story. [3]

It seemed to be "a development of the utmost significance. ... The Allies were still encountering severe resistance and Hitler's plan to retreat into the Bavarian redoubt and to fight on from there was taken seriously," he wrote later.

"We were doing all we could in our German broadcasts to stir the German people into action against their crazy rulers, and the full story of an example of successful revolt, particularly in Bavaria, would be of invaluable assistance to us in our campaign."

Scrambling to catch a lift with a Piper Cub artillery-spotter aircraft, he flew to Augsburg the next morning, enduring anxious moments when he and his pilot, an American major, found themselves alongside Luftwaffe pilots flying in to surrender in large numbers.

They arrived unharmed, but the Bavarian front was not where he expected it to be, and Newsome realised that US troops could not have entered Munich when Gerngross had expected them to.

In fact, a perfect storm had engulfed the FAB's uprising. The Americans had suddenly surged forwards, knocking German frontline troops southwards. The US divisions had then been delayed by the discovery of a vast network of concentration camps around Dachau and one of the Reich's largest prisoner-of-war camps. It meant that while the American forces were doing all they could for the victims of some of the most shocking crimes of the twentieth century, southern Bavaria was filling up with hardened Waffen-SS units, some virtually intact, angry at their crushing defeat and hungry for revenge.

"The (FAB) revolt may have succeeded if only the Americans had arrived in Munich sooner. But at the last minute, the American army had been diverted from its drive on Munich to the town of Dachau and its by then infamous concentration camp.... the first concentration camp most of the Americans had ever encountered," according to American historian and academic Jeffrey Gaab.[4]

For the American soldiers, the horror was compounded by the fact that they had never expected to make these discoveries and barely understood what they were. The first to witness signs of the barbarity were soldiers from the 12th Armoured Division, who stumbled upon a pile of some 500 charred, naked corpses, near the town of *Hurlach* on April 27. Unknowingly – there were no outward signs other than the corpses - they had entered an outlying Dachau subcamp known as *Kaufering IV,* one of eleven in the Kaufering complex, scattered around *Landsberg am Lech*, 40 miles west of Munich.

Hidden beneath their feet was a vast underground death factory, but all they could see on this first encounter was a large clearing in a wood, barbed wire and the corpses. Most of the prisoners had been evacuated to the main camp, while those too weak to work were left behind to be murdered. The guards had shut them in their barracks, nailed up the doors, doused them in petrol and set them alight before fleeing.[5]

Similar atrocities at concentration camps in northern areas of the Reich had been reported in the press, but these were the first witnessed by the troops of the Seventh Army. There had been no warning of what lay in store; the Allies had known of the main concentration camp but not of the existence of the chain of *Arbeitskommandos* (labour camps) around it. They housed factories built in vast concrete underground bunkers for protection from Allied bombing raids. Even the barracks that housed the prisoners were half-buried and camouflaged so that air reconnaissance would not detect them.

These subcamps, satellites of the main 20-acre Dachau site, were built from 1943 onwards to make use of slave labour. By the end of the war there were a total of 123. Those forced to work in the subterranean factories were moved out from the main camp to sleep in huts close by that were also partly buried and offered little shelter in the winter. The harsh conditions caused terrible suffering and life expectancy was little more than six months.

It was in these vast, concealed underground bunkers in *Kaufering IV* that Hitler's 'breakthrough' fighter plane, the jet-powered Messerschmitt Me 262, was to be built. Nicknamed *Sturmvogel* ("Storm Bird"), the aircraft developed in the early years of the war was faster and more heavily armed than any Allied fighter plane.[6]

Believing they would need slave labour to help build the 'Alpine Fortress', the Nazis had dragged those able to walk with them when they fled. Those too weak or sick to be 'death marched' into the mountains were to be murdered, but the speed of the Americans' advance meant the guards had run out of time, leaving many survivors to tell their tales.

The discoveries traumatised many of the young American soldiers. "I didn't even know what we were looking at. It took me a while to realise it was a pile of dead bodies," one said.[7] Another horrified witness spoke of how they "saw bodies spewed over six acres" and "the odour could almost be seen".

Among the troops was a 26-year-old US counter-intelligence officer from a Jewish family, Jerome David Salinger. The young writer, who would become famous for his 1951 novel, *The Catcher in the Rye,* was so deeply affected by the experience that – like so many – he had to be hospitalised for several weeks when the war ended.

He commented later: "You never really get the smell of burning flesh out of your nose entirely, no matter how long you live".[8] Outraged American commanders ordered the soldiers into the nearby town to round up all the male civilians they could find at gunpoint and stand over them while they buried the dead prisoners.

In one report, the Nazi camp *Kommandant* was forced to lie among a pile of corpses while townspeople walked past, spitting on him.[9]

Several other US divisions heading towards Munich that day had broken off their advance to do what little they could for the pitiful, "walking skeletons" they stumbled across and document the crimes they found. Only when the prisoners explained what the camp really was, and showed how it worked, did they understand what the large furnaces were for.

The American 'push' on Munich was being ambushed on all fronts that day. The 14th Armoured Division learned only hours before a fierce, pitched battle outside the town of *Moosburg* that what German troops there were desperate to prevent them from reaching was the Reich's largest prisoner of war camp. A total of more than 116,000 PoWs were housed in huts originally built to hold no more than 10,000.

They included 27 Red Army generals, the sons of four American generals and a number of war correspondents - yet none of the US troops had even known of its existence. The risk of PoWs being caught in cross-fire meant the Americans were forced to fight without artillery back-up and only succeeded in liberating the camp on April 29.[10]

The only division with any sense of what lay ahead was the one Newsome had attached himself to. Taking advantage of the panic in the camp, a prisoner had escaped from Dachau on April 26, and had managed to reach the advancing US forces. He was able to describe what was happening in the camp, and urged action before the thousands left behind were slaughtered.[11]

Giesler had, in fact, initially ordered that all 32,000 prisoners left behind should be shot. When camp guards protested, he demanded poison be put in the prisoners' soup instead.[12]

But this was prevented after the FAB broadcasts inspired the two rebel groups to seize control of the town hall and most of the SS guards fled. [13]

Newsome recalled later how his experiences in Dachau – "that ghastly place" – remained "deeply graven on my memory", including witnessing the open doors of what became known as the Buchenwald-Dachau death train. This was a covered goods train revealing the rotting corpses of 2,310 prisoners left to starve to death. "Corpses lay on the road beside the railway line. Dogs gnawed at them while villagers, on their way to the shops, passed by unconcerned."

After filing his reports, he pressed on with the soldiers to Munich. Meanwhile, the contact he had arranged to meet there to help him find Gerngross, had already arrived. US 7th Army press officer Ernest Langendorf had set off, like Newsome, on April 30 to find the fighting on the Bavarian front line to organise press coverage of the capture of Munich.

He soon overshot the predicted battle lines marked on his map but, thinking the fighting lay ahead, pressed on along the deserted roads and streets. Before he knew it, the towers of Munich's famous *Frauenkirche* loomed up in front of him and he found himself in the city's main square.

By a remarkable twist of fate, Langendorf, a 38-

year-old German who had been forced into exile in the US for attacking Hitler in a newspaper article, became the "first American into Munich", arriving though he did not know it, at the same hour as Hitler committed suicide.[14]

It was a cold, grey day and the historic square was deserted. He and his sergeant, Wolfgang Rabinow, tried the door of the City Hall but it was locked. Then suddenly a cheering crowd came streaming out of the building's cellar, the women clutching bunches of cowslips and primroses with which they covered the Americans' jeep. At 4.15pm, *Oberrechtsrat* (City Council Senior Legal Advisor) Dr Michael Meister handed over the keys of the City Hall to commanders of the US 7th Army. Eisenhower had already telegraphed the 7th Army to congratulate them on "the seizure of Munich, the cradle of the Nazi beast".

Eight days later, just as Victory in Europe Day celebrations were beginning, a man lay dying at a small military hospital in the village of *Bischofswiesen* in the shadow of Hitler's "Eagle's Nest" mountain retreat near Berchtesgaden. Five days earlier he had been treated by doctors after he and his wife had taken poison in a suicide pact that left them seriously ill but failed to kill them. Both recovered and were discharged.

The next day, in warm Spring sunshine they strolled calmly into a wood overlooking the shores of Lake Hintersee near the village of *Ramsau*. There, the man shot his wife dead. Then he turned the gun on himself, but succeeded only in inflicting a severe head wound. Found by passers by who heard the shots, he was returned to the hospital but died from the wound. For Gauleiter Paul Giesler, the "ghastly business" was finally over.

Dr Karl Scheid, whose wife, Lotte, accompanied Gerngross' pregnant wife, Brigitte, to a mountain hideaway before the uprising began. Dr Scheid, aged 38, was shot in the back by SS guards after they waved him through a checkpoint. He was on his way to the U.S. troops to peacefully surrender the town where he was a hospital doctor. He was described by a colleague as a "sworn enemy of National Socialism". Picture courtesy of Markus Wrba, Rechtsanwalt, Tergernsee.

12

Upon reaching Munich, Newsome set out to find Gerngross. He knew that the American troops' delayed arrival would have left the FAB men at serious risk, and so on reaching US Army headquarters was relieved to find a tall, impatient figure fitting Gerngross' description pacing up and down in front of a desk. The dark-haired Bavarian, who, Newsome felt, bore "a strong resemblance to [British Foreign Secretary] Anthony Eden"[1] was towering over a young Counterintelligence Corps (CIC) officer and engaged in a testy exchange in perfect English.

After leaving the farm at *Binsham*, Gerngross had reported immediately to the US 3rd Army, but was held for screening after his identity papers were dismissed as 'stolen'. "The real Rupprecht Gerngross is hanging from a lamppost in Munich's *Ludwigstraße*" the CIC officer told him, having heard that morning's German news broadcasts.[2] Gerngross' plea that he urgently needed to reach his pregnant wife Brigitte and baby daughter in their remote mountain hide-out before the SS cut no ice.

The smock and lederhosen-attired Gerngross

aroused instant suspicion when he strode purposefully into the American offices speaking fluent English. Especially when he pulled a manifesto for a political revolution out of his hunter's rabbit-bag. The scene was recorded by American intelligence officer Harry Lindauer in his military report.

"The impression he makes is certainly not that of a German Army Captain," wrote the bemused Lindauer, "nor that of a leader of an underground movement... he would pass inspection easily though, as a sophisticated member of the 'International Set'. Speaks excellent English. He appeared in peasant's garb and in possession of a complete set of forged papers."

Harry's son, David, who later wrote a book about his father's wartime experiences, [12] said his father's description denoted a "tall, urbane man who spoke several languages, and who could be easily placed into a high-society cocktail party, whether it be in Wiesbaden, Monte Carlo, London, or Park Avenue, New York, and not seem out of place in any of those venues. The term 'jet-set' might apply."

It was hardly surprising. With the terrible images of the heaps of rotting corpses still fresh in the minds of American officers, every German was now suspect. There were no longer any doubts about the savagery of the regime, and to Gerngross' disbelieving captors, it seemed clear that any open revolt against the Nazis would have been tantamount to suicide.

It is a theme examined by Holocaust and World War II historian Professor Rebecca Boehling, who looked at the role of the US military government in Munich. Witnessing the mass-murders at Dachau "made the idea of internal German anti-fascism seem unfathomable," she concluded in her book about postwar Germany, *A Question of Priorities Democratic Reforms and Economic Recovery*.[4]

Fortunately for Gerngross, two American officers he had helped smuggle out of the PoW camp at *Moosburg* were tracked down and vouched for him. Newsome then agreed to drive him into the mountains to rescue his wife and baby daughter, interviewing him along the way.

This is how the British journalist and the man behind the anti-Hitler FAB rebellion now found themselves sitting in a jeep, heading into SS-controlled territory, the two of them embarking on what Newsome called "a mad adventure" together, armed only with Luger pistols.

"It was with some trepidation that I set out," Newsome, 39, recalled with a degree of understatement. "Strong SS forces still held the area. Nor did I view the prospect of a ten or eleven-hour trek up the mountains without some qualms... However, if Frau Gerngross, who was going to have a baby in September, could do it, so could I.... I couldn't with any self-respect get out of it, so off we went."

Shortly after passing the last American patrol, they heard artillery and machine-gun fire coming from the next valley. With the Führer's death still unconfirmed, it was clear that the SS had no intention of giving up the fight, and Gerngross feared the worst for his family. Yet their first encounter was with a small, dispirited cluster of retreating German soldiers just a few miles from Himmler's chalet at *Valepp* on the shores of the Lake Schliersee.

Thinking quickly, Newsome, who was wearing "full British battledress", sprang from the jeep and demanded their weapons. After a brief stand-off, the Germans did what they were told. Newsome and Gerngross put the best pistols in their rucksacks and threw the rifles and machine-guns into the ravine.

Gerngross' priority was rescuing Brigitte but he clearly could not resist the temptation to hold his old enemies to account if an opportunity presented itself along the way. Tired and hungry by the evening, they came across a small inn on the Austrian side of the old border at *Erzherzog-Johann-Klause*, with "hundreds of Germans camped around it in bivouacs, together with piles of mortars, machine guns and grenades, with an air of enormous exhaustion and defeat hanging over them".

They threaded their way cautiously through the milling German troops, and the entire inn fell silent as they walked through the door.

Leaving Newsome with a group of German officers, Gerngross went to order food and drink but returned in a state of excitement, having identified someone he thought was a member of the Gestapo's sister organisation, the *Sicherheitsdienst* (SS Field Security Police) – the most hated of all Nazi organisations.

"Ask him for his papers," demanded Gerngross impetuously, pointing to the shifty-looking man, dressed in civilian clothes.

He was, indeed, a member of Himmler's *Sicherheitsdienst*. "Gerngross was all for taking him outside and shooting him," Newsome recalled. The journalist wisely declined both this suggestion and another, even more hair-raising proposal that they take the SS man with them when they left and execute him some distance away. "There were, we knew, SS troops not far away... They had not given up the fight. In any case, I felt that even an SS man was entitled to a trial," recalled Newsome.

A German officer asked where they were headed and provided them with an amphibious jeep to help them with the river-crossings ahead. But Newsome found being driven along an "excruciatingly narrow and winding track, with a sheer drop of about 50 feet to the stream below... by a particularly sullen-looking German" terrifying. "One twist of the wheel and we should be over the edge... Suppose he was a fanatic, who would like to strike one last blow for the Reich?" he wondered.

To Newsome's relief, they were set down safely and, after negotiating "what seemed to me the sheer mountain face" by 'fullish' moonlight and wading waist-deep in snow, they came within sight of the mountain hut, where Gerngross' wife, daughter and loyal friend Lotte Scheid were in hiding.

Suddenly they spotted three sets of footprints ahead that led up to the hut's door, and it alarmed them enough to get their guns ready. After a low whistle by Gerngross, the door opened slightly and a pistol appeared, a woman's trembling hand holding it. "It's Rupprecht! Gerngross shouted, and the door opened wide to reveal a white-faced Brigitte.

"We went in and sank down into the thick, soft hay... One of the sergeants took a huge cauldron, filled it with snow and put it on the stove... he emptied three bottles of brandy and a packet of sugar into it. That was, I think, the best drink I have ever had," Newsome recalled.

Sipping the grog, Brigitte told excitedly of how she had successfully concealed her identity from three SS men, who came searching for her and, after persuading them her husband was fighting, prepared food, gave them copious amounts to drink and sent them on their way.

The next morning, the party set off home on foot and found their route again took them past the grand chalet owned by Himmler. Spying a powerful Mercedes in the garage, Gerngross summoned the chauffeur and ordered him to drive them back to Munich. Newsome was struck by how the driver was "just the kind of man one would have expected to have been employed by Himmler... a pale, rat-like creature with cruel black eyes and thin lips."

The man at first insisted he could not start the car. Gerngross said he was "sure" he could and pulled out his luger. The chauffeur made several more unsuccessful attempts but said it was "no good". "I'll give you one more chance," said Gerngross and stuck his pistol into the man's ribs. The car started.

They returned to Munich that day in high spirits

and "in great style, stopping at an inn on the outskirts, where we drank a lot of excellent champagne".

The mood of gaiety lasted only as long as it took Gerngross to learn the cost of the FAB's rebellion. The Nazi response had been characteristically brutal and bloody, and while the precise death toll among the group's supporters was unclear, it was certain that the losses had been heavy. With Newsome taking notes, Gerngross set about piecing together what had happened.

The launch of the rebellion had rested on a final reconnaissance of SS units in the city, carried out at 5pm that afternoon. Only one was identified, and on this basis, factory workers were instructed to block roads and railway workers to stop trains to prevent reinforcements coming into the city. The group was confident it had the numbers to hold Munich until the American troops arrived.

But, as Newsome discovered: "Unfortunately, unknown to Gerngross and purely by chance, a strong force of SS had been brought into Munich in the interval between Gerngross' last reconnaissance and the blocking of the roads and railways. This force immediately brought up heavy weapons against the FAB... and there was heavy fighting throughout the night."

The Nordach division of SS had been at full strength that night and moved quickly on the Munich Reichsender radio station after Gerngross returned there from his meeting with Braun, when he discovered that Epp had been set free. Gerngross and a few companions kept the station on the air until 11am on the Saturday morning, but were forced to flee with the SS less than a quarter of a mile away.

It was painful for Gerngross to learn of the tragic fates of the many FAB fighters at the hands of Giesler's forces – especially that of his close friend Caracciola-Delbrück. More grim news was in store when he drove Newsome to Tegernsee to interview Dr Karl Scheid, the husband of his wife's friend, Lotte. There they learned that Wehrmacht soldiers had heard the FAB broadcasts and refused to defend the town, leaving the SS to stage a vain last stand. Newsome was eager to talk to Scheid about his role in the resistance, and particularly his friendship with the 'White Rose' students.

But on reaching *Bad Wiessee*, they learned that Scheid, a hospital doctor, had been shot and wounded in the back by the SS, and been taken to a US military hospital. He had not personally taken part in the uprising but as American troops approached had tried to ensure the safety of patients in the town's many hospitals by negotiating a peaceful surrender.

He had obtained written confirmation that two SS units defending the town would withdraw if US troops held back a threatened bombing raid on the town and he and two companions set off to hand it to American army officials.

The trio were forced to travel on foot because a road bridge had been destroyed. Wearing white armbands and carrying white flags, they passed an SS checkpoint as they headed out of *Bad Wiessee*. On reading the document signed by SS commanders, the men waved them through, only to machine-gun them from behind when they were just over 150 yards away. One was killed outright, but Scheid and his other companion managed to reach the American lines and handed over the written offer.

Sadly, before Gerngross and Newsome could reach him, Scheid died from a bullet lodged in his kidneys on May 4 – the day the U.S. army peacefully liberated the town. The identity of two SS men never came to light despite almost five years of investigations.5

They returned to Munich and, after compiling his broadcast reports, Newsome wrote an article recounting the story of Gerngross and his FAB men for the *Times* newspaper in London. He was told there was great interest in the story and it was destined for the prestigious 'leader page' slot, but the following day nothing appeared.

"I learnt later that... it was thought advisable to have it 'vetted' for policy by the Foreign Office. They (*The Times*) had been asked not to publish it as it was not thought desirable to suggest that there were 'good Germans', Newsome wrote later.

It was the first in a long line of 'disownings' that Gerngross was to suffer.

Munich's Lord Mayor Dr Karl Scharnagl, pictured centre in 1930, a Dachau concentration camp survivor, whose loyalty to the FAB did not waver. Source: Bundesarchiv, Bild 102-09043 / CC-BY-SA 3.0.

13

It had been, wrote Newsome, a "sparkling morning, with the rising sun lighting up the serried ranges of snow-clad peaks" when he and Gerngross trekked from the shepherd's hut down the mountain to Munich. Both believed the future, too, was sparkling bright and they chatted excitedly with the camaraderie that sharing danger engenders.

Newsome's elation was understandable; the war was finally over and his adventure with Gerngross in the mountains had been a success. He would speak of their new-found friendship in a special Victory Day broadcast. "I spent these last two days entirely with Germans, with members of the resistance group of Munich," he said..

"These men and women ... risked torture and death for their political beliefs and faith... they knew... that they were taking a tremendous risk.... none faltered, and, if there are enough young people like these in Germany, then there is great hope for Europe."

Newsome had built up a large and loyal following of listeners for Radio Luxemburg from all over Europe. He was sure the Allies would lease the station from its commercial owners and set up an international broadcasting service reflecting the new order of the world. One serving all nations – victorious, defeated or uninvolved.

For his part, Gerngross believed the FAB's vision of democracy and dignity would now become a reality, and the darkness of 12 years of tyranny lifted.

But neither men's hopes were to be fully realised. As the Allies and the Russians carved up Germany between them, Newsome saw the first signs of a new conflict – one that would become known as the Cold War - emerging. Before him was "the haunting spectre of the might-have-been." There could, he said, "have been a determined effort by the victorious Allies to establish an effective world authority, with a united Europe, as one of its main supports... It was not to be."

Gerngross' hopes were dealt a similar blow. It soon became apparent that he would have no say in how postwar Bavaria was to be organised. To his frustration, the Americans viewed the FAB as a partisan political organisation, rather than one that merely sought a return to democratic rule.

They suspected Gerngross of being in league with the Bavarian monarchist movement, put him on their 'watch-list' and later placed him under house arrest. This meant his phone was tapped and his post intercepted and often held for long periods to be read by military censors, making it hard for him to earn a living as a solicitor at a time when he had a wife and two young children to support.

He was forced to re-qualify and for many years

afterwards found his professional path blocked by those who resented his wartime activities. "We didn't want to found a political party or anything like that," he protested. "The most important thing after the war was to work.... We wanted to try to do our best in our professional jobs to help rebuild our destroyed home country.... But, it is safe to say, the old Nazi judges were still there... and after the war, I suffered a period of bitter financial hardship and had to work hard to earn every Mark in the face of the resistance, often from judges from the old days."[1]

Far from the joyous liberation they had dreamt of, postwar life under US military government was dull and frustrating. Simply moving around the city meant negotiating endless checkpoints requiring fingerprinted ID passes, while curfews made it hard for the old comrades to so much as meet up and relive their exploits over a stein of beer. Even using a bicycle needed extensive authorisation.[2]

Slowly, the restrictions eased, and the American authorities came to acknowledge that, while the FAB uprising had failed from a military point of view, it had hastened the collapse of the Nazi regime in the city, saving both German and Allied lives. Recognising this, the Americans asked if he and his men would be prepared to work with the CIC.

But despite the popular relief that the war was over, many Germans saw active co-operation with the occupying forces as unpatriotic, and Gerngross feared that any help he gave the Americans would be portrayed – particularly by nationalist groups – as proof of his "treachery". [3] Moreover, having mocked the Nazis for their racism, he worried he would be accused of 'hypocrisy' as the US troops were still mostly racially segregated. [4]

Aware, too, that the real work of the FAB was done, he turned the offer down. He and his men agreed, however, to assist the Office of Strategic Services (OSS), precursor of the CIA, with the task of tracking down 'dangerous Nazis' and those behind the Werewolf organisation and, for this, the FAB was given its own office.[5] The relationship, however, was never going to be an easy one.

In Gerngross' view, the Americans failed to understand how hard it had been to operate as a resistance movement under a dictatorship. They found the FAB's complex mixture of loyalties bewildering, and struggled to grasp how its members had fought for the protection of their much-loved 'Fatherland' from its criminal government that had, at one point, at least, been democratically elected. Americans, thought Gerngross, liked to see a "clear winner", while FAB's record was one of successes and failures.

"The Americans already had their own ready-made concept of how the Germans ... should be introduced to democracy", he recalled sadly. "They found the FAB rebellion troublesome in the sense that it failed to include a final battle around Berchtesgaden, with the goal of sending the last Teutons to their Valhalla. Too deeply-embedded was the feeling that all Germans were Nazis." [6]

Another difficulty for Gerngross and his men was that the Americans, feeling their way through the nervous uncertainty of imposing military rule on a people slowly emerging from years of tyranny, were hesitant to publicise a story that hinged partly on saving the city from the annihilation *they*, the Allies, had planned for it.

Glossing over the FAB's role in the capture of the city became part of what was seen as the necessary smoothing of relations between the occupying force and its citizens, and this found a voice in the American press. One American war correspondent went so far as to suggest that the true purpose of the FAB rebellion had been to "create an alibi for old Nazis."[7]

Among those anxious to denigrate Gerngross's achievements were DOLKO members, who had been excluded from the conspiracy because of their pro-Nazi leanings. They had every reason to. Eager to carve out careers for themselves in the new West Germany, the last thing they wanted was to face suspicious questions as to why they had been considered too untrustworthy to be members of the FAB . By dismissing the rebellion as a failure they could protect their own futures.

The story fuelled resentments on another level. When an article in the regional *Bayerische Landeszeitung* newspaper proudly declared: "Munich is the only city in Germany, in which there was a large, united action against the Nazi regime." [8] Other states, jostling for position in the new post-war order, turned a jealous eye and swiftly set about demolishing the claim. Soon Gerngross and his men began to feel almost as isolated as they had been as conspirators.

He felt as if he was surrounded by people on all sides afraid either of what they had done – or what they hadn't. "Everywhere I went I met either former National Socialists, or people with a bad conscience about the fact that they had not done anything and *they,* the ones who had simply stood idly by, were very thick on the ground," he told a friend. [8]

The hostility was hard to shake off. When FAB members met up to celebrate the first anniversary of the uprising in the cocktail bar of Munich's Hotel Carlton, one newspaper criticised the event as "inappropriate" [9]

Yet there were those, like Munich's newly-elected mayor Karl Scharnagl, a Dachau concentration camp survivor, who remained grateful to the FAB and others, whose loyalty and admiration did not waver. Attempts were made to set the record straight. Criticism of the anniversary reunion was dealt a stern rebuke; an anonymous columnist in the Munich newspaper *Streiflicht* (Ray of Light) expressed dismay at those who had condemned the FAB rebellion as oath-breaking, 'treasonous' behaviour: "It is sad when people still don't recognise today who the traitors were in Hitler's country!"[10]

Gerngross and Leiling took further consolation from seeing several of the ideas from FAB's ten-point plan for an interim government appear in the constitution of the new Free State of Bavaria. Some were later incorporated, almost word-for-word, into the 1949 West German constitution. Gerngross felt gratified that the proposals he had been forced to conceal on the back of a Hitler portrait were now accepted as part of the new democratic structure.

Even with scant acknowledgment, he felt a strong sense of pride that he and his men's integrity had remained intact through twelve years of Nazi brainwashing and they had been able to play a part in their country's "spiritual preparation" for democracy.[11]

"We are very proud of the fact that, after all those years of National Socialism with its slogans and rallying cries, despite the indoctrination we had undergone, that we still had the foresight to conceive of what both the Bavarian and the Federal German constitution would contain, all the issues surrounding human dignity and how a state should be ordered: we raised all these points in our ten point plan." [12]

But his primary concern at this point was the financial hardship being suffered by his men in the paralysed city. Finding a house in *Wasserburgstrasse*, he turned it into a FAB 'welfare centre' distributing food and clothing, but this venture quickly fell foul of the occupying forces, who closed it under anti-association laws. The rules were harsh and applied with few exemptions – not even former concentration camp internees were allowed to meet up.[13]

Within weeks of the liberation, the FAB was banned. No specific reason was given at the time, and Gerngross only discovered it years later. Two men, falsely purporting to be FAB members, had crossed a checkpoint to commit a murder.[14]

He appears to have borne all the setbacks with great fortitude, patiently insisting that the project had never been driven by sophisticated political concepts; most followers were pragmatic, humble men, who simply wanted to hasten the end of the war and go back to work in a free society.

"In our ranks there were no desperadoes or 'Hemingway-types', but we wanted more than to simply get by 'unscathed'. Above all we wanted to bring an end to the damage done by the Nazis with their ideology, the inhumanity, the bigotry, the criminal manipulation in the form of public and private life."[15]

Despite the difficulties, the story of the FAB rebellion began to be retold through the trials of Nazi criminals . Gerngross was summoned as a witness, and doubtless found it galling to listen to the defences offered up to the court.

Salisco was described in court by men he led as "irascible and aggressive". Eye-witnesses who were in the bunker that night also told post war trials that several Nazi officials there were 'blind drunk'.[16] Yet the SA-Sturmbannführer was treated with bizarre leniency when he claimed to have offered Caracciola-Delbrück the chance to flee.

In his defence, he testified that he had delayed the execution until Giesler would let him put it off no longer. He then claimed to have offered the Major the chance to escape. This, though, he said, was turned down. He then gave Caracciola-Delbrück his word that he "would not suffer unnecessarily"; he promised to put a bullet in the back of his head after he had faced the firing squad. This was sufficient for the court to decide that there was "no evidence of any base motive" and, in this case, Salisco was only found guilty of aiding and abetting manslaughter[17], though he eventually received a life sentence for a string of other crimes.

Witness after witness revealed the rage, revenge and bloodlust of those in Giesler's bunker that morning. Hübner was said to have proclaimed loudly there would be "no peace until a body was hanging from every lamppost in the *Ludwigstraße*". At this Giesler and SA-*Oberführer* August Flemisch had been delighted and were heard to say with gleeful approval: "*Now* we'll get things in order!"[18]

Hübner was said to have hanged or shot up to 200 people in the last days of the war – executions, the court ruled, that were not lawful as his judgements were "pure acts of despotism and, in reality, represented orders to murder".[19] But for these, and for the executions of the officers who failed to blow up the bridge at Remagen, he was sentenced to merely four years imprisonment and died twenty years later after a comfortable retirement, aged 68.

The terror of the last Nazi victims was recounted, with witnesses recalling seeing people who were told they had been sentenced to death being dragged from room to room by guards searching for the 'flying court martial' officials. When, in the chaos, none could be found, they were thrown back into their cell and locked up again. [20] Gerngross also learnt for the first time how his mother, who had refused to speak to him of her ordeal that day, had stood up "with an iron will to Salisco and Giesler when she was being grilled." [21] And despite having just been told "out of spite" that her son, Rupprecht, was dead. [22]

Some FAB members emerged unscathed from their hiding places, knowing nothing of the subterranean bloodbath that had taken so many of their men. Several only learnt of the fate Giesler had drawn up for them weeks after they returned to their daily lives. A piece of paper thrust into the hands of Wieninger by a busy CIC official turned out to be his death sentence, personally signed by the Gauleiter. The haunting experience left him speechless: "I shook with fear when I read that piece of paper. It was an order to have me executed."[23]

The trials also disclosed the fate of Epp, whose whereabouts had been unknown to the FAB men. He had not entirely escaped the finger of suspicion. After reports filed to Hitler's bunker stated his role in the uprising had been 'unclear', he had been despatched to the Chief of the Reich Main Security Office Ernst Kaltenbrunner in Salzburg.

Few details of his long interrogation in the presence of the feared, scar-faced Waffen-SS general are known but soon afterwards, Epp was hospitalised, suffering from a heart condition. On May 9 1945, a hospital clerk alerted the CIC that he was a patient and he was sent to a prison camp to await trial at Nuremberg. Before it could take place, Epp died in the camp on January 31 1947, aged 79.

As fear of the Nazis subsided, ordinary men such as lorry drivers, who, literally, knew where the bodies were buried, came forward and six corpses were exhumed from the Perlach Forest, just outside the city. One driver told how *Volkssturm* men loaded "two long boxes covered with sheet metal" onto the back of his lorry. They told the driver the boxes contained "valuable machinery parts" but there was also a tarpaulin from which he saw the feet of a corpse protruding.

Noting his alarm, the *Volkssturm* men reassured him it was the body of a captured "looter".[24] The driver now knew for certain he had been ferrying the corpses of three murder victims to their burial site in the forest that day.

Only on rare occasions where courts failed, did natural justice take its course. The corrupt Christian Weber, who had been released by the FAB men when they were forced to flee the Radio Munich station, was rounded up by American soldiers, who tracked him down at his lakeside villa on May 10. He was loaded, along with other prisoners into an open-back lorry, which skidded off the road and overturned on its way to a prison camp. The corpulent 62-year-old was thrown out, suffering fatal head injuries and was buried in a mass grave.[25]

As the post-war *Wirtschaftswunder* (economic miracle) propelled West Germany to a brighter future, many Germans felt it best to draw a veil over the shameful murders that took place in the last, chaotic days of the war, preferring to consign them to oblivion.

However, their grisly evidence remained. A body found in 1959 near the city's Cornelius Bridge led police to re-open files from the end of the war. It turned out to be that of a young Nazi Werewolf involved in a shoot-out with two FAB members on April 30 1945. They had returned fire as he fled – and only discovered fourteen years later that one of their bullets had actually killed him. The FAB men were deemed to have acted in self-defence and spared a trial.[26]

And, as time wore on, bystanders haunted by harrowing scenes for decades, felt the need to come forward to confide details. On the fiftieth anniversary, a priest in the town of *Giesing* received a letter from an eye-witness who described seeing SS-men firing shots and demanding white bedsheets hung from windows be removed. When a tramworker came out of his house to speak to them, he was shot and died from his wounds two days later. A second man, a special constable, who ran to his aid, was also shot. A third, who went to help also came under fire and died of his wounds. [27]

Gerngross was determined his men's bravery should not be consigned to oblivion along with the country's dark Nazi past but, after one interview shortly before the first anniversary, a group of former FAB members accused him of "intolerable vanity" for putting himself centre-stage arguing that the rebellion had been a 'community action'.[28]

Twenty years passed without any further acknowledgement. Then, in June 1965, it was suggested that Gerngross might be honoured with an award -*"München leuchtet"* (Munich lights the way) - for outstanding service to the city. In a sign of the conflicting emotions still rife in post-war West Germany, a great deal of unease was voiced and, when a city archive director ruled that "an objective judgement" as to "the way in which the *Freiheitsaktion Bayern* had contributed to the ending of the war in the Munich area" could not be made due to the "lack of primary sources", the idea was swiftly abandoned.[29]

Ten years later, on his 60th birthday, the authorities backed down. The decision was reversed and Gerngross *was* finally awarded the medal in its gold (highest) form.[30] There was talk of 20 FAB members being issued with similar gold coins and a commemorative stamp being produced but none of this happened. Those for whom the FAB would always be "treasonous oath-breakers" had not gone away.

A 1975 film about the rebellion starring a well-known German actor, who discovered the story and played Gerngross himself, was savaged by critics. "Trash Nazis" ran the scornful headline in *Die Zeit* newspaper, congratulating all the viewers who "managed to sleep through it".[31] Stern magazine weighed in, calling it "cheesy" and said it had been made by "beat-pounding apologists for the *Wehrmacht*" who were "depicting reality through rose-tinted spectacles".[32]

When the Munich underground was modernised later that decade, notices renaming a square *Münchner Freiheit* (Munich Freedom) in the FAB's honour in 1947, were removed during construction work and 'lost'. It took a year-long campaign for replacements to be approved. Thirty six years after the uprising, the injustice was redressed – Gerngross and surviving FAB members witnessed the unveiling of a bronze plaque in the square stating that it bore that name because the FAB "together with other resolute citizens had, by their resistance to the Nazi tyranny, prevented senseless bloodshed".[33]

There was further disappointment when Berlin opened a memorial centre dedicated to the German resistance in 1980. Gerngross attended the opening but criticised the museum for failing to mention the Freedom Action of Bavaria despite a small display focusing on 'Last Minute Resistance' featuring himself and his interpreters but with a reference only to a 'Freedom Action Munich'. [34] A similar display could be viewed by visitors in 2019 but the photograph of Gerngross had been removed and it still did not include any reference to the FAB.

A request for material on the Freedom Action of Bavaria drew blank looks from guides, despite the museum boasting of an "extensive library of 5,000 photographs, books, biographies and other works on all aspects of the resistance to National Socialism." One member of staff eventually found a small entry in a paperback book stored on one of the lower floors. The *Lexicon des Widerstandes 1933-45* (Lexicon of the Resistance) by Peter Steinbach and Johannes Tuchel outlines the uprising noting simply that FAB 'gave people the courage to take action against the Nazis'.

Gerngross nevertheless continued to work tirelessly to keep the memory of his fellow resistance fighters alive. He gave talks to schoolchildren, volunteered for educational roles in the *Bundeswehr*, the West German army, and was made a Reserve Army major in 1960. In the 1980s, he was appointed to the board of the *Zentralverband demokratischer Widerstands- und Verfolgten-Organisationen in Bayern* (Central Association of democratic Resistance and Persecution-Organisations in Bavaria), an umbrella organisation set up to campaign, among other things, for the victims of Nazi injustice.

The least he wanted was a memorial to five of his fellow resistance fighters, including Caracciola-Delbrück who lost their lives – at the spot where they fell. A request was duly made for a simple, commemorative plaque to the "last victims of the Nazi terror in Munich" to be placed on the outside of what had become the Bavarian Agricultural Ministry building for passers-by to see.

This was rejected by ministry officials, who insisted it be placed, instead, in the *inner* courtyard on the south side of the building citing the danger of attacks by "radical political groups".[35] Left with little choice, the committee agreed. The unveiling ceremony was attended by Gerngross 12 years before he died in 1996, aged 80.[36]

Die Partei ist zerbrochen!

Es ist soweit. . . .   Es lebe der Friede!

Helft alle mit unnötiges Blutvergießen zu vermeiden!

Vermeidet den Bruderkrieg Deutsche gegen Deutsche.

Die Besetzung ist unvermeidlich.

Wir wollen Frieden ohne Blutvergießen!

Wir fordern daher auf zu:

    1. Nichtbefolgung aller Wiederstandsbefehle!

    2. Beseitigung aller Panzersperren!

    3. Entschlossene Sicherstellung aller gefähr-
        lichen Elemente!

Sichert Leben, Hab u. Gut durch weiße Fahnen

Friede, Freiheit, Leben!
FAB für unser Bayern! FAB

One of the original leaflets printed at the newspaper offices by FAB rebels on the night of the uprising. It calls for 'Peace without bloodshed' and an end to the 'fratricidal war of Germans fighting Germans'. It tells people 'The (Nazi) Party is broken... make safe all dangerous members... occupation is unavoidable. To protect lives and property, put out white flags... Peace, Freedom, Life!... for our Bavaria!" Courtesy of Josef Höhl, Vorsitzender der ARGE für Heimatkunde Grafing, Germany.

Death march survivors stand outside a barn at Waakirchen, 37 miles south of Dachau, after their Nazi guards fled and soldiers of the US 522nd Field Artillery Battalion – the only segregated Japanese-American unit in Germany at the time – discovered them and found them shelter. Many of the soldiers' own relatives had been interned in America during the war. Picture courtesy of the US Holocaust Museum.

14

One question Newsome had asked Gerngross before they shook hands on parting was whether the rebellion had been worth the loss of so many close colleagues. There was no easy answer.

For most surviving FAB members, though, the answer was – and remained – clear. Wieninger, one of the founding members of today's Christian Social Union party in Germany, wrote: "It cost lives.... 42 people died ... but, through their sacrifice, many thousands were saved.

"It is a fact," he declared "that the planned bombardment was halted... In the Autumn of 1946, the then American city commander Eugene Keller in the presence of Lord Mayor Karl Scharnagl confirmed that, because of the FAB uprising, the planned raid of 2,400 bomb attacks was stood down. Munich and its people were spared much terror and suffering by this." American sociologist Howard Becker, who worked for the propaganda unit of the OSS reported that the US bombing attack planned for Munich had been "on a 500-plane scale". [1]

The then Archbishop of Munich, Cardinal Michael

von Faulhaber, echoed this sentiment. "The FAB can without presumption make the claim that, through their uprising, much blood and misery was avoided."

Journalist Bernhard Ücker, who chronicled Munich's post-war years, agreed. "Even if it was last-minute... these people [the FAB]... ensured that the [already] ruined city of Munich did not become a battlefield razed to the ground... and who knows how many thousands of people were saved from what the gentlemen of the "brown Apocalypse" [the Nazis] planned.[2]

Becker pointed out that the FAB's disruption of the Nazis' defence plans for Munich closed off the "only remaining corridor to the Alpine Fortress" and asked: "Does this account for Hitler's last-minute decision to stay in Berlin for the 'Twilight of the Gods'?[3]

Gerngross certainly considered news of his rebellion reaching the Führer's ears in the hours before his death as a great victory. "It is recorded in the annals of war, the diaries of the army's High Command that Hitler, while still alive and before he had begun preparing to end his life, had knowledge of the uprising in the so-called 'capital of the movement'. That was for us a great triumph".[4]

Others, estimating the overall death toll to be far higher than 42 (some believe as many as 200 lost their lives) issued damning indictments. German historian Joachim Brückner said: "The FAB hugely underestimated the war situation, the powers the NS regime still had available to it, and overestimated their own chances. The attempted rebellion was insufficiently prepared and amateurish... It accomplished nothing and only produced unnecessary casualties."[5] British historian Ian Kershaw assessed the FAB uprising simply as a "brave mistake".[6]

But many of these judgements came before the in-depth research carried out by Munich historian Veronika Diem. Only when her work was published in 2013 did it become clear that 440 people – far more than previously thought – had been at the centre of the FAB uprising that night and that its radio appeals inspired more than a thousand others to rise up against the Nazis in 79 different acts of rebellion.[7]

Finally, her research in American military archives revealed the truth about the FAB's contact with American intelligence services. Few had believed Gerngross' claim to have been in prior contact with the Allies.

Clearly, there are justified criticisms. Gerngross's goal of 'the best possible outcome with the least possible bloodshed' was not achieved. Neither can it be argued that his stated pledge to "stop Germans killing Germans" was fulfilled, although he could not have foreseen that the Americans would be delayed in the vital hours when the FAB had expected to be able to count on them. Fewer people might have lost their lives if the rebels had grasped the fact that the Nazis' terror apparatus was still virtually intact.

The unexpected transfer of a key contact at the last minute in Nuremberg was a blow that meant their 'Bavarian' uprising could only cover half the region. And, as Diem points out, they had failed to cultivate any contacts in the higher military, the Waffen-SS or around Giesler, who by 1944 controlled the *Volkssturm*.[8]

She says it remains unclear whether the FAB really understood the potency of their rallying calls over the radio that night and knowingly took risks to mobilise as many followers as possible.[9] Certainly, unlike the Valkyrie plotters, who represented a social elite with expectations of alternative leadership, Gerngross and his men were less worldly and may have underestimated the impact they would have.

"It touched a raw nerve in the population," wrote Diem, "gave momentum to end the long, agonising wait and undertake something to save one's own community from feared destruction.

"But the actions taken in fulfilling this need followed no logical pattern and because of all the passion bound up with it, risks were overlooked..." concluded Diem.[10] She admits that Gerngross was "a personality who, long after his death, will provoke conflicting reactions." Whilst a lack of sources means a "definitive judgement" cannot be made, she calls for "the memory of these people (the estimated 1,400 in total who took part) and the 58 victims, who were murdered, to be a future point of departure for an appropriate perception of the Freedom Action of Bavaria".[11]

Gerngross conceded that people who joined in the uprising were swept up with the elation of the night. "We knew that there were many opponents of National Socialism among the miners in Penzberg...

and in one of the few truly spontaneous acts there they seized the town hall by themselves and deposed the mayor.... They attached a great deal to the significance of our broadcast."

But he remained adamant that the FAB did not exaggerate their claims to have seized power. "From the moment the governor (Epp) was with us and until he made clear he did not want to carry out the surrender, we were, to all intents and purposes, in control of the city," he said. "We had control of City Hall, we had occupied the command bunker in Pullach, we had seized the general headquarters (of the army), there was no longer a police constabulary, so we had control both of the city and the state of Bavaria with the *Freiheitsaktion Bayern* at work everywhere."[12]

In the broadcasts, listeners were urged to 'remove' the Nazis. The word in German (*beseitigen*) is ambiguous. It can mean 'remove' them from office or could be taken to mean 'eradicate' or kill them. Most listeners took it as a call, at the very least, to arrest and lock up their local party officials.

Gerngross believed the ferocity of the Nazi reprisals may have reflected the troops' despairing realisation that the Führer's promised haven of safety – the 'Alpine Fortress' – was a mirage. As they reached the River Inn with still no idea of where this sought-after haven lay, it surely began to dawn on even hardened Nazis that they had fallen for Goebbel's last big lie. The 'fortress' simply did not exist.

Seeing, at that very moment, white bedsheets

flapping from windows or hearing church bells heralding glorious victory for the despised enemy and their own shameful defeat, was too much to bear and they vented their unconstrained fury.

Gerngross acknowledged the extent of the tragedy. "We lost around 40 people in this way.... courageous men who inspired people to hoist white flags and tragically became casualties. ...And then, obviously, along with the retreating troops every possible Nazi formation came into the area reporting for duty, many from Berlin, transfixed the entire time by the thought of the Alpine Fortress, which never existed."[13]

One FAB supporter revealed how dangerous even the last hours of war could be. He was threatened with being shot when he tried to stop a bridge being blown up in Dachau even though the gunfire of U.S. troops could be heard in the distance. "People accused us of putting up no or, too little, resistance to the regime but even on the very day, on which, just a few hours later, the Americans marched into Dachau, showing resistance put you in mortal danger." [14]

But the FAB had dared to dream on a grand scale at a time when so many Germans stayed passive. They risked their lives and saved those of others by refusing to play safe, and simply sit the war out. Around one and a half thousand people in total all over Bavaria took part in acts of rebellion, many of them peaceful and successful.

The choice of Epp as a figurehead had always been controversial. General Franz Halder, who was imprisoned in Dachau for conspiracy in the wake of the Valkyrie plot, had warned that Epp was "too indecisive and, in fact, too old". Lawyer Otto Leibrecht, one of the original members of Gerngross' parents' *Deisenhofen* circle, who had fled the Gestapo to Switzerland, was horrified at the choice. Epp's political mindset was "heavily imbued with National Socialism" and he was "absolutely unsuitable", he told them.[15]

Yet, it is clear that Epp had enough sympathy with the resistance fighters to arouse suspicion among Hitler's inner circle and, after Sperr's arrest, he was all they had. Gerngross had been prepared to hold Epp at gunpoint to announce a surrender but Caracciola-Delbrück assured them Epp had "signalled" that he would agree to it[16], not realising that, in the final hour of reckoning, the old commander's loyalties to Hitler could not be shifted.

The critical judgements of the FAB seem harsh when set against the gratitude expressed by those such as Dachau death march survivor Ferdinand Zilinsky.

In a letter to a newspaper from his native Czechoslovakia in 1957, he wrote: "There were 3,000 of us being driven into the unknown by a strong force of the *SS-Hauptscharführer* (highest SS rank of chief squad leader) in snow and rain, hungry and soaked through... [then], as we reached *Bad Tölz*, there was a great nervousness among the SS guards. We were brought to a halt and took cover in woodland close to the roadside. The SS were running around helplessly and barely took any notice of us.... The reason was the broadcasts of Captain Gerngross.

"The SS kept us camped in the woods for 48 hours... Without orders, they could not decide what to do with us...in this way we won 48 precious hours, while the American army advanced and we were freed on May 1.

"Had we not won those 48 hours, it is questionable whether we would have lived to experience that liberation. This courageous man, Captain Gerngross indirectly saved the lives of around 3,000 innocent concentration camp internees."[17]

Gerngross never accepted that the failure of the rebellion to meet all its aims meant it was a mistake. The goal – noble if ambitious – was to save their city from destruction, avoiding mass civilian deaths and, to an important degree, it succeeded. By their example, believed Gerngross, they showed the world that not every German was a blind follower of Nazism.

The greater failure, Gerngross felt, would have been not going through with the plan. "As a political gesture we wanted not only to save the city from catastrophe, but also to show that there was a real resistance in Germany and for years we had risked our lives and for us to suddenly back out... That would have been humiliating for us, we would have felt deeply ashamed." [18] Two years before Gerngross died, he attended a conference honouring the memory of both the French and German wartime resistance movements organised by Germany's Schiller Institute. He told the audience: "This we knew at the time: in a dictatorship nothing could be done with democratic methods... nothing could be gained with silent opposition or a clenched fist in the pocket.

"The activists were only bound by human trust... [We] knew: anyone who put himself in danger, loses his life." But Gerngross said he had always kept uppermost in his mind the words of the German poet Friedrich Schiller, that: "If you do not put your life at risk, you will never have won life."[19]

His resentment at the way the FAB movement was effectively erased, first from the history books and then from the common memory, was shared by those who had fought alongside him. In 2001, former White Rose member Dr Jürgen Wittenstein was invited to give a speech at the opening of an exhibition on the German resistance movement at the University of California.

He was "dismayed", he said, to find no mention on the displays of the *Freiheitsaktion Bayern*, for whose uprising he had risked his life as a soldier smuggling supplies of weapons from the Italian Front, having asked to be transferred there to escape the Gestapo.

To amend this glaring inaccuracy, he pointedly tore up the speech he had written and instead told the story of Gerngross' men declaring: "The Freedom Action of Bavaria conducted the only successful military putsch against the Hitler regime. By this action, it saved Munich, which Hitler had ordered to be "defended to the last man," from complete destruction.

"His announcement of the end of the Nazis in Munich led many German soldiers to desert the lost cause and the US forces arriving in Munich on 30

April experienced virtually no resistance when taking the city."[20]

Wittenstein was not alone in wanting to set the record straight. Author and journalist Felix Heidenberger, who wrote a book based partly on the FAB story, lamented that Gerngross had been 'almost completely forgotten' when he was a 'beacon of hope' in the darkness of Nazi Germany. He believed Munich could have easily been razed to the ground in the same way as Warsaw and Stalingrad. "It remains a fact that Munich was not as badly destroyed as other cities and that there was no 'bomb inferno' in the last days. The air-raids were actually called off because of Gerngross' broadcasts."[21]

History's judgement of the FAB uprising on result appears "biased", Diem found, especially when compared to the lionisation of other resistance fighters such as Georg Elser and the White Rose group, whose achievements were viewed more in the context of circumstances and motives than results.[22]

Erich Kästner, author of the much-loved children's novel Emil and the Detectives, was transfixed by Gerngross' voice coming so unexpectedly over the airwaves that night as he sat at his desk in his refuge in the Austrian Tyrol. The writer, who had watched the Nazis burn his books on the bonfires in Berlin, distilled the debate over the FAB putsch into one simple line: "It shows great courage – and trust in God."[23]

Gerngross, himself, gave an even simpler answer. He wrote humbly: "Our chief aim was to end the war without any fanfare and go home... None of us were born 'do-gooders'.[24] We understood that disobedience could be a virtue... and simply followed the path of conscience and stayed committed to the notion of freedom.[25]...... It was the militant path, more wearisome, more dangerous...more thankless[26] but there was no smooth path without being complicit.[27]

"We chose to oppose terror, not simply tolerate it, in the hope we would somehow survive it.[28]... It was about the feeling that the Germans *themselves* did something for their own liberation.[29] It was neither a putsch nor a coup, it was a battle cry for victory."[30]

THE END

The road into Waakirchen, where Japanese-American soldiers did what they could to save those left alive for two days before medical personnel arrived and set up a field hospital. Picture courtesy of the US Holocaust Museum.

Rupprecht Gerngross, pictured here in Munich in 1989, aged 73, recording an interview for the Museum of the House of Bavarian History. Picture courtesy of the museum.

Notes and references

INTRODUCTION:

1. John Toland: *The Last 100 Days: The Tumultuous and Controversial Story of the Final Days of World War II in Europe*, 1966, (reprint 2003) ISBN 0-44092621-1. p. 471

2. Alan Bullock: *Hitler A study in Tyranny*, 1952, reprint 1990, (p.799)

CHAPTER ONE:

1. Interview with Rupprecht Gerngross, Haus der Bayerischen Geschichte Museum, Regensburg, Germany. Verbatim record PR-Nr. 363/1 *Zeitzeugen zur Bayerischen Geschichte* recorded 24/25.4.1989 Munich. (p.1)

2. Interview with Elvira Bodechtel in Münchner Merkur: *Rupprecht Gerngross: Freigeist und Hitler-Gegner*.13.7.15. www.merkur.de/lokales/muenchen-lk/ruprecht-gerngross-deisenhofen-freigesist-hitler-gegner-5238725.html

3. Interview with Rupprecht Gerngross, Haus der Bayerischen Geschichte Museum, Regensburg, Germany. Verbatim record PR-Nr. 363/1 *Zeitzeugen zur Bayerischen Geschichte* recorded 24/25.4.1989

München. (p.2)

4. Rupprecht Gerngross: *"Fasanenjagd" und wie die Münchner Freiheit ihren Namen bekam. Erinnerungen des Dr. Rupprecht Gerngross.* Augsburg: Heidrich, 1995. ISBN 3-930455-92-7. (p.65)

5. *"Fasanenjagd" und wie die Münchner Freiheit ihren Namen bekam. Erinnerungen des Dr. Rupprecht Gerngross.* Augsburg: Heidrich, 1995. ISBN 3-930455-92-7. (p.64)

6. Interview with Rupprecht Gerngross, Haus der Bayerischen Geschichte Museum, Regensburg, Germany. Verbatim record PR-Nr. 363/1 *Zeitzeugen zur Bayerischen Geschichte* recorded 24/25.4.1989 Munich. (p.24)

7. Interview with Rupprecht Gerngross, Haus der Bayerischen Geschichte Museum, Regensburg, Germany. Verbatim record PR-Nr. 363/1 *Zeitzeugen zur Bayerischen Geschichte* recorded 24/25.4.1989 München. (p.10)

8. Alan Bullock: *Hitler A study in Tyranny,* 1952, reprint 1990, (p.61)

9. Alan Bullock: *Hitler A study in Tyranny,* 1952, reprint 1990 (p. 63)

10. thirdreichruins.com/tegernsee.htm

11. The New York Times: *The Holocaust just got More Shocking,* by Erich Lichtblau.1.3.2013.

12. Interview with Rupprecht Gerngross, Haus der Bayerischen Geschichte Museum, Regensburg, Germany. Verbatim record PR-Nr. 363/1 Zeitzeugen zur Bayerischen Geschichte recorded 24/25.4.1989 Munich.

(p.19) and Süddeutsche Zeitung of 28.4.1995: *50 Jahre Kriegsende - Widerständler besetzen Rundfunksender* by Klaus Reichold

13. Süddeutsche Zeiting of 28.04.1995: *Geheime Treffen im Hinterzimmer* by Klaus Reichold.

14. Interview with Rupprecht Gerngross, Haus der Bayerischen Geschichte Museum, Regensburg, Germany. Verbatim record PR-Nr. 363/1 *Zeitzeugen zur Bayerischen Geschichte* recorded 24/25.4.1989 Munich. (p.20-21)

15. Interview with Rupprecht Gerngross, Haus der Bayerischen Geschichte Museum, Regensburg, Germany. Verbatim record PR-Nr. 363/1 *Zeitzeugen zur Bayerischen Geschichte* recorded 24/25.4.1989 Munich. (p.21)

16. John Toland: *The Last 100 Days: The Tumultuous and Controversial Story of the Final Days of World War II in Europe*, 1966, reprint (2003) ISBN 0-44092621-1. (p.470)

17. Interview with Rupprecht Gerngross, Haus der Bayerischen Geschichte Museum, Regensburg, Germany. Verbatim record PR-Nr. 363/2 Zeitzeugen zur Bayerischen Geschichte recorded 24/25.4.1989 Munich (p.2) and Nr. 363/1 p.18

18. Veronika Diem: *Die Freiheitsaktion Bayern: ein Aufstand in der Endphase des NS-Regimes*, 2013. Kallmünz/Opf: Verlag Michael Lassleben. ISBN: 9783784730196 (pp.66-7 citing Theodor Duesterberg: *Der Stahlhem und Hitler*, Wolfenbüttel, Hannover 1949. (p.149)

CHAPTER TWO:

1. UPI.com/Archives/1935/03/16Hitler-orders-military-conscription-in-Germany/5124911384073/

2. Interview with Winfried Pöllner, Haus der Bayerischen Geschichte Museum, Regensburg, Germany. *Zeitzeugen Projekt*. Verbatim record of interview with Winfried Pöllner recorded 6.10.2005 Munich. (p.13)

3. Interview with Rupprecht Gerngross, Haus der Bayerischen Geschichte Museum, Regensburg, Germany. Verbatim record PR-Nr. 363/2 *Zeitzeugen zur Bayerischen Geschichte* recorded 24/25.4.1989 Munich (p.9)

4. Interview with Rupprecht Gerngross, Haus der Bayerischen Geschichte Museum, Regensburg, Germany. Verbatim record PR-Nr. 363/2 Zeitzeugen zur Bayerischen Geschichte recorded 24/25.4.1989 Munich. (p.11)

5. Newman, Michael. *Ralph Miliband and the Politics of the New Left*. Merlin Press (2002).(p.22) ISBN 978-0-85036-513-9.

6. Felix Heidenberger: *Mau Yee – Münchner Freiheit – a non-fiction novel*. Berlin: Pro Business GmbH: ISBN: 3-938262-30-3 (p.14)

7. Rupprecht Gerngross: *"Fasanenjagd" und wie die Münchner Freiheit ihren Namen bekam. Erinnerungen des Dr. Rupprecht Gerngross*. Augsburg: Heidrich, 1995. ISBN 3-930455-92-7. (p.65)

8. Joachim Fest: *Plotting Hitler's Death. The German Resistance to Hitler 1933-1945*. Weidenfeld & Nicolson, London. 1994. ISBN: 0 297 81774 4. (p.119)

9. Joachim Fest: *Plotting Hitler's Death The German Resistance to Hitler, 1933-1945*. Weidenfeld & Nicolson, London. 1994. ISBN: 0 297 81774 4. (p.223)

10. Joachim Fest: *Plotting Hitler's Death The German Resistance to Hitler, 1933-1945*. Weidenfeld & Nicolson, London. 1994. ISBN: 0 297 81774 4. (p. 179 citing Horst Mühleisen ed. Helmut Stieff: Briefe (Berlin 1991) 127 Sept 5, 1941: Hans Meier-Wecke, Aufzeichnungen eines Generalstabs-offiziers (1939-1942) (Freiburg 1982), p.121.

11. Joachim Fest: *Plotting Hitler's Death. The German Resistance to Hitler, 1933-1945*. Weidenfeld & Nicolson, London. 1994. ISBN: 0 297 81774 4. (p.116-7 citing Hildegard von Kotze, ed. Heeresadjutant bei Hitler 1938-1943; Aufzeichnungen des Majors Engel (Stuttgart 1974, 68, (entry of Nov. 18, 1939)

12. Anne Nelson: *Red Orchestra: The Story of the Berlin Underground and the Circle of Friends Who Resisted Hitler*. New York. Random House, 2009. ISBN 9781588367990 (p.180)

13. Rupprecht Gerngross: *"Fasanenjagd" und wie die Münchner Freiheit ihren Namen bekam. Erinnerungen des Dr. Rupprecht Gerngross*. Augsburg: Heidrich, 1995. ISBN 3-930455-92-7. (p.12); Interview with Rupprecht Gerngross, Haus der Bayerischen Geschichte Museum, Regensburg, Germany. Verbatim record PR-Nr. 363/2 *Zeitzeugen zur Bayerischen Geschichte* recorded 24/25.4.1989 Munich. (p.24)

14. Interview with Rupprecht Gerngross, Haus der Bayerischen Geschichte Museum, Regensburg, Germany. Verbatim record PR-Nr. 363/2 *Zeitzeugen zur Bayerischen Geschichte* recorded 24/25.4.1989 Munich

(p.25)

15. Felix Heidenberger: *Mau Yee – Münchner Freiheit – a non-fiction novel*. Berlin: Pro Business GmbH: ISBN: 3-938262-30-3 (p.16)

16. Dr. Rupprecht Gerngross: *"Fasanenjagd" und wie die Münchner Freiheit ihren Namen bekam. Erinnerungen des Dr. Rupprecht Gerngross*. Augsburg: Heidrich, 1995. ISBN 3-930455-92-7. (p.12)

CHAPTER THREE:

1. Rupprecht Gerngross: *"Fasanenjagd" und wie die Münchner Freiheit ihren Namen bekam. Erinnerungen des Dr. Rupprecht Gerngross*. Augsburg: Heidrich, 1995. ISBN 3-930455-92-7. (p.48); Walter Ziegler: *Hitler und Bayern*, Verlag der Bayerischen Akademie der Wissenschaften, Munich, 2004 (p.5) citing Max Domarus, Hg., *Hitler.Reden und Proklamationen 1932-45*, Bd 1, Würzburg 1962. (p.353)

2. rarehistoricalphotos.com/nazi-christmas-party-hitler-1941

3. Interview with Winfried Pöllner. Haus der Bayerischen Geschichte Museum, Regensburg, Germany. *Zeitzeugen-Projekt,* Verbatim record des Zeitzeugen-Interview recorded 6.10.2005, Munich. (p.6.)

4. Rupprecht Gerngross: *"Fasanenjagd" und wie die Münchner Freiheit ihren Namen bekam. Erinnerungen des Dr. Rupprecht Gerngross*. Augsburg: Heidrich, 1995. ISBN 3-930455-92-7. (p.23).

5. Rupprecht Gerngross: *"Fasanenjagd" und wie die Münchner Freiheit ihren Namen bekam. Erinnerungen*

des Dr. Rupprecht Gerngross. Augsburg: Heidrich, 1995. ISBN 3-930455-92-7. (p.29).

6. Interview with Rupprecht Gerngross, Haus der Bayerischen Geschichte Museum, Regensburg, Germany. Verbatim record PR-Nr. 363/2 *Zeitzeugen zur Bayerischen Geschichte* recorded 24/25.4.1989 Munich (p.17)

7. Rupprecht Gerngross: *"Fasanenjagd" und wie die Münchner Freiheit ihren Namen bekam. Erinnerungen des Dr. Rupprecht Gerngross.* Augsburg: Heidrich, 1995. ISBN 3-930455-92-7. (p.75)

8. The Moosburger Stalag – Stalag VIIA (Kreigsgefangenen-Mannschafts-Stammlager VII-A) (en.wikipedia.org/wiki/Stalag_VII-A)

9. Rupprecht Gerngross: *"Fasanenjagd" und wie die Münchner Freiheit ihren Namen bekam. Erinnerungen des Dr. Rupprecht Gerngross.* Augsburg: Heidrich, 1995. ISBN 3-930455-92-7. (p.50)

10. Rupprecht Gerngross: *"Fasanenjagd" und wie die Münchner Freiheit ihren Namen bekam. Erinnerungen des Dr. Rupprecht Gerngross.* Augsburg: Heidrich, 1995. ISBN 3-930455-92-7. (p.145)

11. Veronika Diem: *Die Freiheitsaktion Bayern: ein Aufstand in der Endphase des NS-Regimes,* 2013. Kallmünz/Opf: Verlag Michael Lassleben. ISBN: 9783784730196 (p.63 citing conversation with Willi Klein, aged 97, who was a French interpreter at Moosburg from Spring 1941 until Summer 1943.

12. Rupprecht Gerngross: *"Fasanenjagd" und wie die Münchner Freiheit ihren Namen bekam. Erinnerungen des Dr. Rupprecht Gerngross.* Augsburg: Heidrich, 1995.

ISBN 3-930455-92-7. (p.50)

13. Rupprecht Gerngross: *"Fasanenjagd" und wie die Münchner Freiheit ihren Namen bekam. Erinnerungen des Dr. Rupprecht Gerngross*. Augsburg: Heidrich, 1995. ISBN 3-930455-92-7. (pp.53-4)

14. Rupprecht Gerngross: *"Fasanenjagd" und wie die Münchner Freiheit ihren Namen bekam. Erinnerungen des Dr. Rupprecht Gerngross*. Augsburg: Heidrich, 1995. ISBN 3-930455-92-7. (p.51)

15. Veronika Diem: *Die Freiheitsaktion Bayern: ein Aufstand in der Endphase des NS-Regimes*, 2013. Kallmünz/Opf: Verlag Michael Lassleben. ISBN: 9783784730196 (p.68 citing Karl Ude: *Soldat in der verdunkelten Stadt*. In Proebst, Hermann u.a. (Hrsg)*: Denk ich an München. Ein Buch der Erinnerungen*. München 1966. (p.257)

16. Interview with Rupprecht Gerngross, Haus der Bayerischen Geschichte Museum, Regensburg, Germany. Verbatim record PR-Nr. 363/3 *Zeitzeugen zur Bayerischen Geschichte* recorded 24/25.4.1989 Munich. (p.5)

17. Interview with Rupprecht Gerngross, Haus der Bayerischen Geschichte Museum, Regensburg, Germany. Verbatim record PR-Nr. 363/3 *Zeitzeugen zur Bayerischen Geschichte* recorded 24/25.4.1989 Munich. (pp.5-6)

CHAPTER FOUR:

1. Rupprecht Gerngross: *"Fasanenjagd" und wie die Münchner Freiheit ihren Namen bekam. Erinnerungen des Dr. Rupprecht Gerngross*. Augsburg: Heidrich, 1995.

ISBN 3-930455-92-7. (pp. 94-5, p. 101)

2. Interview with Rupprecht Gerngross, Haus der
   Bayerischen Geschichte Museum, Regensburg,
   Germany. Verbatim record PR-Nr. 363/6 *Zeitzeugen zur
   Bayerischen Geschichte* recorded 24/25.4.1989 Munich.
   (pp.18-19)

3. Interview with Rupprecht Gerngross, Haus der
   Bayerischen Geschichte Museum, Regensburg,
   Germany. Verbatim record PR-Nr. 363/3 *Zeitzeugen zur
   Bayerischen Geschichte* recorded 24/25.4.1989 Munich.
   (p.19)

4. https://en.wikipedia.org/wiki/Rupprecht,_Crown_Prin
   ce_of_Bavaria citing Jonathan Petropoulos: *Royals and
   the Reich: The Princes von Hessen in Nazi Germany.*
   Oxford University Press, 2006. ISBN: 9780195161335

5. Interview with Rupprecht Gerngross, Haus der
   Bayerischen Geschichte Museum, Regensburg,
   Germany. Verbatim record PR-Nr. 363/2 *Zeitzeugen zur
   Bayerischen Geschichte* recorded 24/25.4.1989 Munich.
   (pp.22-3)

6. The Guardian: *Nazi loyalist and Adolf Hitler's devoted
   aide: the true story of Eva Braun* by Kate Connolly
   14.2.2010 citing Heike Goertemaker*: Eva Braun: Life
   with Hitler* published by Knopf ISBN9780307742605

7. Felix Heidenberger: *Mau Yee – Münchner Freiheit – a
   non-fiction novel.* Berlin: Pro Business GmbH: ISBN: 3-
   938262-30-3 (pp.19-20)

8. Interview with Elvira Bodechtel in Münchner Merkur:
   Rupprecht Gerngross: Freigeist und Hitler-Gegner.
   13.7.15 (www.merkur.de/lokales/muenchen-
   lk/ruprecht-gerngross-deisenhofen-freigesist-hitler-

gegner-5238725.html)

9. Veronika Diem: *Die Freiheitsaktion Bayern Ein Aufstand im April 1945 und seine Folgen: Inauguraldissertation zur Erlangung des Doktorgrades der Philosophie and der Ludwig-Maximilians-Universität München.* 2011 (p.145 citing Report of Leo Heuwing 3.2.1946 IfZ, ZS/A4/6, also foreword of Robert von Werz's *Freiheitsaktion Bayern*, February 1946 IfZ, ZS/A4/7

10. Interview with Rupprecht Gerngross, Haus der Bayerischen Geschichte Museum, Regensburg, Germany. Verbatim record PR-Nr. 363/6 *Zeitzeugen zur Bayerischen Geschichte* recorded 24/25.4.1989 Munich. (pp.22-3)

11. Interview with Rupprecht Gerngross, Haus der Bayerischen Geschichte Museum, Regensburg, Germany. Verbatim record PR-Nr. 363/6 *Zeitzeugen zur Bayerischen Geschichte* recorded 24/25.4.1989 Munich. (p.22)

12. Pave the Way Foundation Reveals Evidence of Pope Pius XII's Active Opposition to Hitler, 29.6.2009 as cited in Wikipedia. *Pave the Way Foundation Reveals Evidence of Pope Pius XII's Active Opposition to Hitler* June 2009 at the Wayback Machine, (p.24) (http://www.transworldnews.com/NewsStory.asp x?id=95893&cat=15)

13. Roman Catholic Archdiocese of Munich and Freising website: *Franz Sperr – Gesandter Bayerns in Berlin* by Fred G. Rausch. January. (https://www.erzbistum-muenchen.de/cms-media/media-11033820.pdf)

14. Interview with Rupprecht Gerngross, Haus der

Bayerischen Geschichte Museum, Regensburg, Germany. Verbatim record PR-Nr. 363/6 *Zeitzeugen zur Bayerischen Geschichte* recorded 24/25.4.1989 Munich. (p.23)

15. Joachim Fest: *Plotting Hitler's Death. The German Resistance to Hitler, 1933-1945.* Weidenfeld & Nicolson, London. 1994. ISBN: 0 297 81774 4. (p.295) (Count Fritz-Dietlof von der Schulenburg)

16. William L. Shirer: *The Rise and Fall of the Third Reich: A History of Nazi Germany.* Simon & Schuster, New York, 1990. ISBN: 13:9780671728687 (pp. 1070-1071)

17. Interview with Rupprecht Gerngross, Haus der Bayerischen Geschichte Museum, Regensburg, Germany. Verbatim record PR-Nr. 363/6 *Zeitzeugen zur Bayerischen Geschichte* recorded 24/25.4.1989 Munich. (pp.21-2)

18. Joachim Fest: *Plotting Hitler's Death. The German Resistance to Hitler, 1933-1945.* Weidenfeld & Nicolson, London. 1994. ISBN: 0 297 81774 4. (p.236) citing Fabian von Schlabrendorff: *Offiziere Gegen Hitler*, Fischer Bücherrei, 1959 (p.109)

CHAPTER FIVE:

1. Don Allen Gregory: *After Valkyrie: Military and Civilian Consequences of the Attempt to Assassinate Hitler.* McFarland. 2018. ISBN: 9781476634470 citing former Hitler Youth member and later historian Alfons Heck. (p.18)

2. Internet Archive: *Full text of Adolf Hitler's last Radio Speech* 30.1.1945 in archive.org/stream/AdolfHitlerLastRadioSpeechJan301

945/AdolfHitlerLastRadioSpeechJan301945_djvu.tx

3. Rupprecht Gerngross: *"Fasanenjagd" und wie die Münchner Freiheit ihren Namen bekam. Erinnerungen des Dr. Rupprecht Gerngross.* Augsburg: Heidrich, 1995. ISBN 3-930455-92-7. (p.78)

4. Ian Kershaw: *Hitler 1889-1936: Hubris.* Allen Lane, The Penguin Press. London 1998. ISBN: 0-713-99229-8 (pp.158-9) and Alan E. Steineis in *Kristallnacht 1938.* Harvard University Press, 2009 (p.80)

5. Rupprecht Gerngross: *"Fasanenjagd" und wie die Münchner Freiheit ihren Namen bekam. Erinnerungen des Dr. Rupprecht Gerngross.* Augsburg: Heidrich, 1995. ISBN 3-930455-92-7. (pp.76-7)

6. *Daily Mail* 13.12.2019 How the Nazis found Solace in Suicide by Tony Rennell citing Florian Huber: Promise me you'll shoot yourself by Allen Lane, London. 2019 (https://www.dailymail.co.uk/news/article-7791213/Citizens-took-lives-face-shame-retribution-Hitler-defeated.html)

7. Rupprecht Gerngross: *"Fasanenjagd" und wie die Münchner Freiheit ihren Namen bekam. Erinnerungen des Dr. Rupprecht Gerngross.* Augsburg: Heidrich, 1995. ISBN 3-930455-92-7. (p.39)

8. Veronika Diem: *Die Freiheitsaktion Bayern: ein Aufstand in der Endphase des NS-Regimes*, 2013. Kallmünz/Opf: Verlag Michael Lassleben. ISBN: 9783784730196 (p.164 citing Becker, Winfried: *Franz Sperr und sein Widerstandskreis* in Rumschöttel, Hermann und Ziegler, Walter (hrsgb): *Franz Sperr und der Widerstand gegen den Nationalsozialismus in Bayern* (Zeitschrift für Bayerische Landesgeschichte

Reihe B Beiheft 20 München 2001 pp. 83-159)

9. Interview with Rupprecht Gerngross, Haus der Bayerischen Geschichte Museum, Regensburg, Germany. Verbatim record PR-Nr. 363/6 *Zeitzeugen zur Bayerischen Geschichte* recorded 24/25.4.1989 Munich. (pp.29) and Rupprecht Gerngross: *"Fasanenjagd" und wie die Münchner Freiheit ihren Namen bekam. Erinnerungen des Dr. Rupprecht Gerngross.* Augsburg: Heidrich, 1995. ISBN 3-930455-92-7. (p.44)

10. Rupprecht Gerngross: *"Fasanenjagd" und wie die Münchner Freiheit ihren Namen bekam. Erinnerungen des Dr. Rupprecht Gerngross.* Augsburg: Heidrich, 1995. ISBN 3-930455-92-7. (p.45) and Veronika Diem: *Die Freiheitsaktion Bayern: ein Aufstand in der Endphase des NS-Regimes*, 2013. Kallmünz/Opf: Verlag Michael Lassleben. ISBN: 9783784730196 (pp. 398-414 citing citing *Abschliessender Tatsachenbericht der FAB* (Concluding Report of the FAB): BayHStA, Abteilung IV, Handschriftensammlung 2347

11. Nigel Jones: *Countdown to Valkyrie*. Frontline Books, London. 2008. ISBN: 978-1-84832-508-1. (p.266)

12. Joachim Fest: *Plotting Hitler's Death. The German Resistance to Hitler, 1933-1945.* Weidenfeld & Nicolson, London. 1994. ISBN: 0 297 81774 4. (pp. 269-70)

13. Interview with Rupprecht Gerngross, Haus der Bayerischen Geschichte Museum, Regensburg, Germany. Verbatim record PR-Nr. 363/4 *Zeitzeugen zur Bayerischen Geschichte* recorded 24/25.4.1989 Munich. (p.26)

14. Karl Wieninger: *In München erlebte Geschichte*, Strumberger, München, 1985. ISBN: 9783921193211.

(p.89)

15. Veronika Diem: *Die Freiheitsaktion Bayern: ein Aufstand in der Endphase des NS-Regimes*, 2013. Kallmünz/Opf: Verlag Michael Lassleben. ISBN: 9783784730196 (p.160 citing the diaries of Joseph Goebbels. Part II Diktate 1941-5 Band 9 July – September).

16. Veronika Diem: *Die Freiheitsaktion Bayern: ein Aufstand in der Endphase des NS-Regimes*, 2013. Kallmünz/Opf: Verlag Michael Lassleben. ISBN: 9783784730196 (p.163 citing Annex 'B' to G-2 Periodic Report No. 100 Headquarterws XXI Corps 23.4.45 NARA 407/427/III. Corps/3297)

17. Rupprecht Gerngross: *"Fasanenjagd" und wie die Münchner Freiheit ihren Namen bekam. Erinnerungen des Dr. Rupprecht Gerngross*. Augsburg: Heidrich, 1995. ISBN 3-930455-92-7. (pp.134-5)

18. Rupprecht Gerngross: *"Fasanenjagd" und wie die Münchner Freiheit ihren Namen bekam. Erinnerungen des Dr. Rupprecht Gerngross*. Augsburg: Heidrich, 1995. ISBN 3-930455-92-7. (p.62)

19. Interview with Rupprecht Gerngross, Haus der Bayerischen Geschichte Museum, Regensburg, Germany. Verbatim record PR-Nr. 363/4 *Zeitzeugen zur Bayerischen Geschichte* recorded 24/25.4.1989 Munich. (p.29)

20. Ian Kershaw: *Hitler 1936-45: Nemesis*. Allen Lane, The Penguin Press, London, 2000. ISBN: 0-713-99229-8 (p. 567)

21. Interview with Rupprecht Gerngross, Haus der Bayerischen Geschichte Museum, Regensburg,

Germany. Verbatim record PR-Nr. 363/3 *Zeitzeugen zur Bayerischen Geschichte* recorded 24/25.4.1989 Munich. (p.14)

22. William Shirer: *The Rise and Fall of the Third Reich*, Simon and Schuster, New York, 1960. ISBN: 9780606030380 (pp. 1103-5)

23. Rupprecht Gerngross: *"Fasanenjagd" und wie die Münchner Freiheit ihren Namen bekam. Erinnerungen des Dr. Rupprecht Gerngross*. Augsburg: Heidrich, 1995. ISBN 3-930455-92-7. (p.31)

24. Rebecca Boehling: *A Question of Priorities: Democratic Reforms and Economic Recovery in Postwar Germany*. Berghahn Books, U.S. 1996. ISBN: 978-1-57181-0359 (p.106 citing Michael Schattenhofer (ed.) *Chronik der Stadt München 1945-1948* (Munich 1980. p.43)

25. Rupprecht Gerngross: *"Fasanenjagd" und wie die Münchner Freiheit ihren Namen bekam. Erinnerungen des Dr. Rupprecht Gerngross*. Augsburg: Heidrich, 1995. ISBN 3-930455-92-7. (p.71)

CHAPTER SIX:

1. D.K.R. Crosswell in *"Beetle: The Life of General Walter Bedell Smith."* American Warriors Series. 2010. University Press of Kentucky. ISBN: 97808123136585. p.872 citing a letter to his wife February 1945.

2. Interview with Rupprecht Gerngross, Haus der Bayerischen Geschichte Museum, Regensburg, Germany. Verbatim record PR-Nr. 363/3 *Zeitzeugen zur Bayerischen Geschichte* recorded 24/25.4.1989 Munich. (p.26)

3. Interview with Rupprecht Gerngross, Haus der Bayerischen Geschichte Museum, Regensburg, Germany. Verbatim record PR-Nr. 363/3 *Zeitzeugen zur Bayerischen Geschichte* recorded 24/25.4.1989 Munich. (pp.26-7)

4. Rupprecht Gerngross: *"Fasanenjagd" und wie die Münchner Freiheit ihren Namen bekam. Erinnerungen des Dr. Rupprecht Gerngross*. Augsburg: Heidrich, 1995. ISBN 3-930455-92-7. (p.45) and Interview with Rupprecht Gerngross, Haus der Bayerischen Geschichte Museum, Regensburg, Germany. Verbatim record PR-Nr. 363/3 *Zeitzeugen zur Bayerischen Geschichte* recorded 24/25.4.1989 Munich. (p.27)

5. Rupprecht Gerngross: *"Fasanenjagd" und wie die Münchner Freiheit ihren Namen bekam. Erinnerungen des Dr. Rupprecht Gerngross*. Augsburg: Heidrich, 1995. ISBN 3-930455-92-7. (p.74)

6. Veronika Diem: *Die Freiheitsaktion Bayern: ein Aufstand in der Endphase des NS-Regimes*, 2013. Kallmünz/Opf: Verlag Michael Lassleben. ISBN: 9783784730196 (pp.80-1 citing an unpublished manuscript entitled, *"Die Widerstandsbewegung in Bayern 1933-1945"* thought to be written by Braun, himself, around the beginning of 1948, Sammlung Familie Braun BayHStA, MK 54120)

7. Veronika Diem: *Die Freiheitsaktion Bayern: ein Aufstand in der Endphase des NS-Regimes*, 2013. Kallmünz/Opf: Verlag Michael Lassleben. ISBN: 9783784730196 (p.405 *citing Abschliessender Tatsachenbericht der FAB* (Concluding Report of the FAB): Veronika Diem: *Die Freiheitsaktion Bayern Ein Aufstand im April 1945 und seine Folgen:*

Inauguraldissertation zur Erlangung des Doktorgrades der Philosophie and der Ludwig-Maximilians-Universität München. 2011 (pp. 117-8 citing Report of Jakob Feller of 09.03.1946. IfZ, ZS/A4/6)(BayHStA, Abteilung IV, Handschriftensammlung 2347).

8. Veronika Diem: *Die Freiheitsaktion Bayern: ein Aufstand in der Endphase des NS-Regimes*, 2013. Kallmünz/Opf: Verlag Michael Lassleben. ISBN: 9783784730196 (p.404 citing *Abschliessender Tatsachenbericht der FAB* (Concluding Report of the FAB): (BayHStA, Abteilung IV, Handschriftensammlung 2347

9. Veronika Diem: *Die Freiheitsaktion Bayern Ein Aufstand im April 1945 und seine Folgen: Inauguraldissertation zur Erlangung des Doktorgrades der Philosophie and der Ludwig-Maximilians-Universität München*. 2011 (pp.93-4 citing Report of Hans Betz of 07.071947. IfZ, ZS/A$/ and p.403)

10. Interview with Rupprecht Gerngross, Haus der Bayerischen Geschichte Museum, Regensburg, Germany. Verbatim record PR-Nr. 363/4 *Zeitzeugen zur Bayerischen Geschichte* recorded 24/25.4.1989 Munich. (p.14) and Rupprecht Gerngross: *"Fasanenjagd" und wie die Münchner Freiheit ihren Namen bekam. Erinnerungen des Dr. Rupprecht Gerngross*. Augsburg: Heidrich, 1995. ISBN 3-930455-92-7. (p.131)

CHAPTER SEVEN

1. Ian Kershaw: *The End: Hitler's Germany 1944-45*. Allen Lane, London 2011. ISBN: 9780713997163. (p. 311, citing Bundesarchiv Berlin/Lichterfelde R3/1618,fo.22 re

Führer Vorführung 12.4.45)

2. Rupprecht Gerngross: *"Fasanenjagd" und wie die Münchner Freiheit ihren Namen bekam. Erinnerungen des Dr. Rupprecht Gerngross*. Augsburg: Heidrich, 1995. ISBN 3-930455-92-7. (p.118 citing AZ: 1a Nr. 6671/45. Number 4 of the deputy General Command VII)

3. Ian Kershaw*: The End: Hitler's Germany 1944-45*. Allen Lane, London 2011. ISBN: 9780713997163. (p.320 citing the report of Gauleiter Karl Holz of Franconia 17.4.45)

4. Veronika Diem: *Die Freiheitsaktion Bayern: ein Aufstand in der Endphase des NS-Regimes*, 2013. Kallmünz/Opf: Verlag Michael Lassleben. ISBN: 9783784730196 (p.73 citing the Washington Post obituary of 22.3.2000 for Sidney John Leigh, who was shot down over the Netherlands and http://www.92ndma.org/missions/loss43728.htm

5. As named in Felix Heidenberger: *Mau Yee – Münchner Freiheit – a non-fiction novel*. Berlin: Pro Business GmbH: ISBN: 3-938262-30-3 (p.55) However, Gerngross later recalled his name as Mac Mamara in *"Fasanenjagd" und wie die Münchner Freiheit ihren Namen bekam. Erinnerungen des Dr. Rupprecht Gerngross*. Augsburg: Heidrich, 1995. ISBN 3-930455-92-7. (p.88).

6. Veronika Diem: *Die Freiheitsaktion Bayern: ein Aufstand in der Endphase des NS-Regimes*, 2013. Kallmünz/Opf: Verlag Michael Lassleben. ISBN: 9783784730196 (p.119 citing Report of M11 Team 536 G, Headquarters 86th Infantry Dvision to S-2, 342nd Infantry 24.04.1945 and Report No. 20 Headquarters III Corps, Office of the ACCF S), G-2, M11 Team 449-G to Assistant Chief of Staff G-2 25.04.1945. NARA,

407/427/III. Corps/3297)

7. Veronika Diem: *Die Freiheitsaktion Bayern Ein Aufstand im April 1945 und seine Folgen: Inauguraldissertation zur Erlangung des Doktorgrades der Philosophie and der Ludwig-Maximilians-Universität München*. 2011 (p.119 citing Report of MII Team 536 G, Headquarters 86th Infantry Division to S-2, 342nd Infantry 24.04.1945. NARA, 407/427/III. Corps/3297).

8. Veronika Diem: *Die Freiheitsaktion Bayern: ein Aufstand in der Endphase des NS-Regimes*, 2013. Kallmünz/Opf: Verlag Michael Lassleben. ISBN: 9783784730196 (p.119 citing report of Jakob Feller of 09.03.1946. IfZ, ZS/A4/7 and the foreword of *"Freiheitsaktion Bayern"*, *Diary Notes of Dr. Robert von Werz*, February 1946 IfZ, ZS/A4/7)

9. Rupprecht Gerngross: *"Fasanenjagd" und wie die Münchner Freiheit ihren Namen bekam. Erinnerungen des Dr. Rupprecht Gerngross*. Augsburg: Heidrich, 1995. ISBN 3-930455-92-7. (p.88)

10. Rupprecht Gerngross: *"Fasanenjagd" und wie die Münchner Freiheit ihren Namen bekam. Erinnerungen des Dr. Rupprecht Gerngross*. Augsburg: Heidrich, 1995. ISBN 3-930455-92-7. (p.16, p. 99)

11. Interview with Rupprecht Gerngross, Haus der Bayerischen Geschichte Museum, Regensburg, Germany. Verbatim record PR-Nr. 363/4 *Zeitzeugen zur Bayerischen Geschichte* recorded 24/25.4.1989 Munich. (p.15)

12. Rupprecht Gerngross: *"Fasanenjagd" und wie die Münchner Freiheit ihren Namen bekam. Erinnerungen*

des Dr. Rupprecht Gerngross. Augsburg: Heidrich, 1995.
ISBN 3-930455-92-7. (p.88)

13. Howard Becker: *The Nature and Consequences of Black Propaganda.* In: American Sociological Review Volume 14 Number 2 (1949) Pp.221-235 (p.230)

14. Veronika Diem: *Die Freiheitsaktion Bayern Ein Aufstand im April 1945 und seine Folgen: Inauguraldissertation zur Erlangung des Doktorgrades der Philosophie and der Ludwig-Maximilians-Universität München.* 2011 (p. 132 citing *Memorandum from Chief MO Branch, OSS,* Lieutenant Colonel John S. Roller to Colonel Kenneth D. Mann and David Williamson 05.04.1945, NARA, 226/139/113/1569 and p.134 citing *Preface* by Lieutenant Colonel John S. Roller of 'Hagedorn'. *Edited Seclections from Radio Scripts Aimed at the Morale Subversion of the German People During the Final Phase of the Third Reich* (February-April 1945) by Dr Hans J. Rehfisch 01.06.1945. NARA, 226/92/588/1.

15. Veronika Diem: *Die Freiheitsaktion Bayern Ein Aufstand im April 1945 und seine Folgen: Inauguraldissertation zur Erlangung des Doktorgrades der Philosophie and der Ludwig-Maximilians-Universität München.* 2011 (p.164)

16. Veronika Diem: *Die Freiheitsaktion Bayern Ein Aufstand im April 1945 und seine Folgen: Inauguraldissertation zur Erlangung des Doktorgrades der Philosophie and der Ludwig-Maximilians-Universität München.* 2011 (p.130 citing *Memorandum of Information for the Joint U.S. Chiefs of Staff from OSS-Acting Director G. Edward Buxton,* June 1945. NARA,226/99/19/1)

17. Veronika Diem: *Die Freiheitsaktion Bayern Ein Aufstand im April 1945 und seine Folgen: Inauguraldissertation zur Erlangung des Doktorgrades der Philosophie and der Ludwig-Maximilians-Universität München.* 2011 (p.137 citing an interview with Drs Gerngross, Leiling and Jacobsen 13-15.06.1945 in a *Report on Black Operations in Today's Germany* by Howard Becker, Edmund Reiss and Rudolf Weiss 13.07.1945. NARA, 226/92/587/41).

18. Ian Kershaw*: The End: Hitler's Germany 1944-45.* Allen Lane, London 2011. ISBN: 9780713997163. (*Preface* xxi)

19. Rupprecht Gerngross: *"Fasanenjagd" und wie die Münchner Freiheit ihren Namen bekam. Erinnerungen des Dr. Rupprecht Gerngross.* Augsburg: Heidrich, 1995. ISBN 3-930455-92-7. (pp.68-9). Veronika Diem in *Die Freiheitsaktion Bayern: ein Aufstand in der Endphase des NS-Regimes*, 2013. Kallmünz/Opf: Verlag Michael Lassleben. ISBN: 9783784730196 reports that the hut lay midway between Erzherzog-Johann-Klause on the Bavarian border and the Guffert mountain in the Tyrol. (p.147)

20. Rupprecht Gerngross: *"Fasanenjagd" und wie die Münchner Freiheit ihren Namen bekam. Erinnerungen des Dr. Rupprecht Gerngross.* Augsburg: Heidrich, 1995. ISBN 3-930455-92-7. (p.82)

21. Rupprecht Gerngross: *"Fasanenjagd" und wie die Münchner Freiheit ihren Namen bekam. Erinnerungen des Dr. Rupprecht Gerngross.* Augsburg: Heidrich, 1995. ISBN 3-930455-92-7. (pp.88-9)

22. Rupprecht Gerngross: *"Fasanenjagd" und wie die Münchner Freiheit ihren Namen bekam. Erinnerungen des Dr. Rupprecht Gerngross.* Augsburg: Heidrich, 1995.

ISBN 3-930455-92-7. (p.71)

23. Interview with Rupprecht Gerngross, Haus der
Bayerischen Geschichte Museum, Regensburg,
Germany. Verbatim record PR-Nr. 363/4 *Zeitzeugen zur
Bayerischen Geschichte* recorded 24/25.4.1989 Munich.
(p.17)

24. Rupprecht Gerngross: *"Fasanenjagd" und wie die
Münchner Freiheit ihren Namen bekam. Erinnerungen
des Dr. Rupprecht Gerngross.* Augsburg: Heidrich, 1995.
ISBN 3-930455-92-7. (p.85).

25. Interview with Rupprecht Gerngross, Haus der
Bayerischen Geschichte Museum, Regensburg,
Germany. Verbatim record PR-Nr. 363/4 *Zeitzeugen zur
Bayerischen Geschichte* recorded 24/25.4.1989 Munich.
(p.19)

26. Veronika Diem: *Die Freiheitsaktion Bayern: ein
Aufstand in der Endphase des NS-Regimes,* 2013.
Kallmünz/Opf: Verlag Michael Lassleben. ISBN:
9783784730196 (pp.172-3 citing reports of Rudolf
Decker of 23.03.1946 and Max Heigl of 11.03.1946. IfZ,
ZS/A4/6).

27. Rupprecht Gerngross: *"Fasanenjagd" und wie die
Münchner Freiheit ihren Namen bekam. Erinnerungen
des Dr. Rupprecht Gerngross.* Augsburg: Heidrich, 1995.
ISBN 3-930455-92-7. (pp.90-1)

28. Veronika Diem: *Die Freiheitsaktion Bayern Ein
Aufstand im April 1945 und seine Folgen:
Inauguraldissertation zur Erlangung des Doktorgrades
der Philosophie and der Ludwig-Maximilians-
Universität München.* 2011 (p.138 citing Memorandum
from Chief MO-Branch to Chief SI Branch 20.05.1945.

NARA, 226/139/113/1569 and p.135 citing MO-Operation Capricorn, Script 22, 'Heraus aus der Apathie' 21.03.1945. NARA, 226/92/588/1).

CHAPTER EIGHT:

1. *"Freiheits-Aktion Bayern 1945"*. Report by Dr Rupprecht Gerngross and Dr Ottheinrich Leiling. Nachlass Gerngross 14. BayHStA.

2. Ian Kershaw: *The End: Hitler's Germany 1944-45*. Allen Lane, London 2011. ISBN: 9780713997163. note 6 Soenke, Neitzel: Abgehoert, Deutsche Generale in Britische Kriegsgefangenschaft, 1942-45, Berlin pp 210-212 English language edition, *Tapping Hitler's Generals: Transcripts of Secret Conversations, 1942-5*, Barnsley, 2007 pp 156-8)

3. Rupprecht Gerngross: *"Fasanenjagd" und wie die Münchner Freiheit ihren Namen bekam. Erinne-rungen des Dr. Rupprecht Gerngross*. Augsburg: Heidrich, 1995. ISBN 3-930455-92-7. (p.96)

4. Veronika Diem: *Die Freiheitsaktion Bayern Ein Aufstand im April 1945 und seine Folgen: Inauguraldissertation zur Erlangung des Doktorgrades der Philosophie and der Ludwig-Maximilians-Universität München.* 2011 (p.236 citing the manuscript *"Das Widersprüchliche und das Durchlässige Lebenserinnerungen 1914 bis 1945"* by Friedhelm Kemp 01.05.1995. Sammlung Kemp. BayHStA)

5. Rupprecht Gerngross: *"Fasanenjagd" und wie die Münchner Freiheit ihren Namen bekam. Erinnerungen des Dr. Rupprecht Gerngross*. Augsburg: Heidrich, 1995. ISBN 3-930455-92-7. (p.123)

6. Veronika Diem: *Die Freiheitsaktion Bayern Ein Aufstand im April 1945 und seine Folgen: Inauguraldissertation zur Erlangung des Doktorgrades der Philosophie and der Ludwig-Maximilians-Universität München.* 2011 (p.174 citing reports of Max Heigl 11.03.1946. IfZ, ZS/A4/6).

7. Rupprecht Gerngross: *"Fasanenjagd" und wie die Münchner Freiheit ihren Namen bekam. Erinnerungen des Dr. Rupprecht Gerngross.* Augsburg: Heidrich, 1995. ISBN 3-930455-92-7. (p.97); Felix Heidenberger: *Mau Yee – Münchner Freiheit – a non-fiction novel.* Berlin: Pro Business GmbH: ISBN: 3-938262-30-3 (p.64-5)

8. Felix Heidenberger: *Mau Yee – Münchner Freiheit – a non-fiction novel.* Berlin: Pro Business GmbH: ISBN: 3-938262-30-3 (p.66)

9. Here and following: Dr. Rupprecht Gerngross: *"Fasanenjagd" und wie die Münchner Freiheit ihren Namen bekam. Erinnerungen des Dr. Rupprecht Gerngross.* Augsburg: Heidrich, 1995. ISBN 3-930455-92-7. (p.98ff)

10. *"Aufstand"*: typed report, *Materialsammlung II Buchstabe 3-D.* Nachlass Gerngross 15. BayHStA.

11. *Radioputsch Auf Welle Muenchen*, Nachlass Gerngross 10, BayHStA; Rupprecht Gerngross: *"Fasanenjagd" und wie die Münchner Freiheit ihren Namen bekam. Erinnerungen des Dr. Rupprecht Gerngross.* Augsburg: Heidrich, 1995. ISBN 3-930455-92-7. (p.103)

12. *Zeitungsausschnitte betr. Rupprecht Gerngross 1945-95.* I. Gerngross Nachlass 13. BayHStA.

13. *An autobiography of Harold J Siddall, 1916-1997,* Naval History Homepage, The National Royal Navy

Museum. Stoker Harold Siddall, recalls visits of
translators to Stalag VIIA (Moosburg) in 1943 and how
they built a small radio which they used to listen to BBC
broadcasts. In Chapter 9, he wrote: "enough parts had
been obtained to make a small radio set, put together by
a lad, who was a member of the Royal Engineers...The
aerial was a copper wire poked up the chimney". Naval-
history.net/WW2MemoirAndS009.htm

14. Rupprecht Gerngross: *"Fasanenjagd" und wie die
Münchner Freiheit ihren Namen bekam. Erinnerungen
des Dr. Rupprecht Gerngross*. Augsburg: Heidrich, 1995.
ISBN 3-930455-92-7. (p.100)

15. Interview with Rupprecht Gerngross, Haus der
Bayerischen Geschichte Museum, Regensburg,
Germany. Verbatim record PR-Nr. 363/3 *Zeitzeugen zur
Bayerischen Geschichte* recorded 24/25.4.1989 Munich.
(p.21)

16. Interview with Rupprecht Gerngross, Haus der
Bayerischen Geschichte Museum, Regensburg,
Germany. Verbatim record PR-Nr. 363/5 *Zeitzeugen zur
Bayerischen Geschichte* recorded 24/25.4.1989 Munich.
(p.10)

17. Rupprecht Gerngross: *"Fasanenjagd" und wie die
Münchner Freiheit ihren Namen bekam. Erinnerungen
des Dr. Rupprecht Gerngross*. Augsburg: Heidrich, 1995.
ISBN 3-930455-92-7. (p.100)

18. Noel Newsome: *Giant at Bush House: At the heart of the
radio war: The autobiography of Noel Newsome, Vol 1
1906-45*. The Real Press, Steyning, UK. ISBN:
9781912119974. Chapter 28: *Excursion Behind the
Enemy's Lines*. (p. 425).

19. Rupprecht Gerngross: *"Fasanenjagd" und wie die Münchner Freiheit ihren Namen bekam. Erinnerungen des Dr. Rupprecht Gerngross.* Augsburg: Heidrich, 1995. ISBN 3-930455-92-7. (p.102); Karl Wieninger: *In München erlebte Geschichte*, Strumberger, München, 1985. ISBN: 9783921193211. (p. 90).

20. Felix Heidenberger: *Mau Yee – Münchner Freiheit – a non-fiction novel.* Berlin: Pro Business GmbH: ISBN: 3-938262-30-3 (p.76)

21. Veronika Diem: *Die Freiheitsaktion Bayern: ein Aufstand in der Endphase des NS-Regimes*, 2013. Kallmünz/Opf: Verlag Michael Lassleben. ISBN: 9783784730196 (p.198 citing Letter from Rupert Baumann to Oberregierungsrat Alois Braun 27.02.1946 IfZ, ZS/A4/6).

22. Rupprecht Gerngross: *"Fasanenjagd" und wie die Münchner Freiheit ihren Namen bekam. Erinnerungen des Dr. Rupprecht Gerngross.* Augsburg: Heidrich, 1995. ISBN 3-930455-92-7. (p.102); *Materalsammlung II Buchstabe 3-D*, Nachlass Gerngross 15. BayHStA.

23. Munich Tageszeitung newspaper of 30.05.17 Kriegsende in München – Die letzten Tage vor der Befreiug 1945: https://www.tz.de/muenchen/stadt/kriegsende-in-muenchen-letzten-tage-vor-befreiung-1945-8362831.html

24. *Materalsammlung II Buchstabe 3-D*. Nachlass Gerngross 15. BayHStA.

25. Interview with Rupprecht Gerngross, Haus der Bayerischen Geschichte Museum, Regensburg, Germany. Verbatim record PR-Nr. 363/6 *Zeitzeugen zur Bayerischen Geschichte* recorded 24/25.4.1989 Munich.

(p.31)

26. Rebecca Boehling: *A Question of Priorities: Democratic Reforms and Economic Recovery in Postwar Germany.* Berghahn Books, U.S. 1996. ISBN: 978-1-57181-0359 (p.107 citing Sunday Times of 29.04.1945)

27. Rupprecht Gerngross: *"Fasanenjagd" und wie die Münchner Freiheit ihren Namen bekam. Erinnerungen des Dr. Rupprecht Gerngross.* Augsburg: Heidrich, 1995. ISBN 3-930455-92-7. (p.94)

28. *Materialsammlung II* Buchstabe 3-D. Nachlass Gerngross 15. BayHstA

29. Karl Wieninger: *In München erlebte Geschichte,* Strumberger, München, 1985. ISBN: 9783921193211. (p.86)

30. Interview with Rupprecht Gerngross, Haus der Bayerischen Geschichte Museum, Regensburg, Germany. Verbatim record PR-Nr. 363/6 *Zeitzeugen zur Bayerischen Geschichte* recorded 24/25.4.1989 Munich. (p.7)

31. Annemarie Liebler, *Geschichte der Regierung von Niederbayern,* Herbert Utz Verlag, Munch, 2008, ISBN: 9783831608362 (p.146)

32. Karl Wieninger: *In München erlebte Geschichte,* Strumberger, München, 1985. ISBN: 9783921193211. (p.97)

33. Rupprecht Gerngross: *"Fasanenjagd" und wie die Münchner Freiheit ihren Namen bekam. Erinnerungen des Dr. Rupprecht Gerngross.* Augsburg: Heidrich, 1995. ISBN 3-930455-92-7. (p.43); Veronika Diem: *Die Freiheitsaktion Bayern: ein Aufstand in der Endphase des NS-Regimes,* 2013. Kallmünz/Opf: Verlag Michael

Lassleben. ISBN: 9783784730196 (p.197 citing the copy of a handwritten report by Max Lacher, date unknown, StadtA, Munich, Familien 716)

34. Interview with Rupprecht Gerngross, Haus der Bayerischen Geschichte Museum, Regensburg, Germany. Verbatim record PR-Nr. 363/4 *Zeitzeugen zur Bayerischen Geschichte* recorded 24/25.4.1989 Munich. (p.31)

35. Interview with Rupprecht Gerngross, Haus der Bayerischen Geschichte Museum, Regensburg, Germany. Verbatim record PR-Nr. 363/6 *Zeitzeugen zur Bayerischen Geschichte* recorded 24/25.4.1989 Munich. (pp.26-7)

36. Rupprecht Gerngross: *"Fasanenjagd" und wie die Münchner Freiheit ihren Namen bekam. Erinnerungen des Dr. Rupprecht Gerngross*. Augsburg: Heidrich, 1995. ISBN 3-930455-92-7. (p.120)

37. Rupprecht Gerngross: *"Fasanenjagd" und wie die Münchner Freiheit ihren Namen bekam. Erinnerungen des Dr. Rupprecht Gerngross*. Augsburg: Heidrich, 1995. ISBN 3-930455-92-7. (p.99)

38. Rupprecht Gerngross: *"Fasanenjagd" und wie die Münchner Freiheit ihren Namen bekam. Erinnerungen des Dr. Rupprecht Gerngross*. Augsburg: Heidrich, 1995. ISBN 3-930455-92-7. (pp.100-101)

39. Interview with Rupprecht Gerngross, Haus der Bayerischen Geschichte Museum, Regensburg, Germany. Verbatim record PR-Nr. 363/4 Zeitzeugen zur Bayerischen Geschichte recorded 24/25.4.1989 Munich. (p.29)

40. Interview with Rupprecht Gerngross, Haus der

Bayerischen Geschichte Museum, Regensburg,
Germany. Verbatim record PR-Nr. 363/5 *Zeitzeugen zur
Bayerischen Geschichte* recorded 24/25.4.1989 Munich.
(p.3)

41. Veronika Diem: *Die Freiheitsaktion Bayern: ein
    Aufstand in der Endphase des NS-Regimes*, 2013.
    Kallmünz/Opf: Verlag Michael Lassleben. ISBN:
    9783784730196 (p.179 citing letter from Eduard
    Schirovsky to Rupprecht Gerngross of 14.10.1945
    BayHStA, Nachlass Gerngross 20 and Report of Eduard
    Schirovsky of 23.2.1946 BayHStA, Nachlass Gerngross
    20)

42. Rupprecht Gerngross: *"Fasanenjagd" und wie die
    Münchner Freiheit ihren Namen bekam. Erinne-rungen
    des Dr. Rupprecht Gerngross.* Augsburg: Heidrich, 1995.
    ISBN 3-930455-92-7. (p.122)

43. Rupprecht Gerngross: *"Fasanenjagd" und wie die
    Münchner Freiheit ihren Namen bekam. Erinnerungen
    des Dr. Rupprecht Gerngross.* Augsburg: Heidrich, 1995.
    ISBN 3-930455-92-7. (p.121)

44. Veronika Diem: *Die Freiheitsaktion Bayern: ein
    Aufstand in der Endphase des NS-Regimes*, 2013.
    Kallmünz/Opf: Verlag Michael Lassleben. ISBN:
    9783784730196 (p.196 citing *Freiheits-Aktion Bayern
    1945* by Rupprecht Gerngross and Ottheinrich Leiling
    (around 15.06.1945) BayHStA/Abteilung IV,
    Handschriftensammlung 2347)

CHAPTER NINE

1. *BBC Daily World News Digest No 1747* 30th April 1945
   by The Editor, West Central District Office, New Oxford

Street, WC1. *Materialsammlung*. Gerngross Nachlass 15, BayHStA.

2. Rupprecht Gerngross: *"Fasanenjagd" und wie die Münchner Freiheit ihren Namen bekam. Erinnerungen des Dr. Rupprecht Gerngross.* Augsburg: Heidrich, 1995. ISBN 3-930455-92-7. (p.101)

3. Ian Kershaw: *Hitler 1936-45: Nemesis.* Allen Lane, The Penguin Press, London, 2000. ISBN: 0-713-99229-8 (p. 823)

4. *BBC Daily World News Digest* Part 1, No 2,112 of 29th April 1945. Period Covered: 00.01 Saturday 28th April to 00.01 Sunday 29th April 1945 by The Editor, West Central District Office, New Oxford Street, WC1. *Materialsammlung*. Gerngross Nachlass 15, BayHStA.

5. *BBC Daily World News Digest* Part 1, No 2,112 of 29th April 1945. Period Covered: 00.01 Saturday 28th April to 00.01 Sunday 29th April 1945 by The Editor, West Central District Office, New Oxford Street, WC1. *Materialsammlung*. Gerngross Nachlass 15, BayHStA.

6. Veronika Diem: *Die Freiheitsaktion Bayern: ein Aufstand in der Endphase des NS-Regimes*, 2013. Kallmünz/Opf: Verlag Michael Lassleben. ISBN: 9783784730196 (p.246 citing a letter written by Adolf Hieber to *Oberregierungsrat* Braun 22.03.1946 containing a report into events in the Wehrmacht Command Centre IfZ, ZS/A4/6).

7. Here and following: *BBC Daily World News Digest* Part 1, No 2,112 of 29th April 1945. Period Covered: 00.01 Saturday 28th April to 00.01 Sunday 29th April 1945 by The Editor, West Central District Office, New Oxford Street, WC1. *Materialsammlung*. Gerngross Nachlass 15,

BayHStA.

8. Here and following: Veronika Diem: *Die Freiheitsaktion Bayern: ein Aufstand in der Endphase des NS-Regimes*, 2013. Kallmünz/Opf: Verlag Michael Lassleben. ISBN: 9783784730196 (p.232 citing an extract from the staff diary of the Swiss General Consulate titled: *"Our experiences of the Front at Lake Tegern"* undated Sammlung Wrba.

9. Veronika Diem: *Die Freiheitsaktion Bayern: ein Aufstand in der Endphase des NS-Regimes*, 2013. Kallmünz/Opf: Verlag Michael Lassleben. ISBN: 9783784730196 (p.218 citing an article in the New York Times of 29.4.1945 by Daniel T. Brigham, *"Reich Army Rebels"* The New York Times Vol. XCIV No. 31,872)

10. Veronika Diem: *Die Freiheitsaktion Bayern: ein Aufstand in der Endphase des NS-Regimes*, 2013. Kallmünz/Opf: Verlag Michael Lassleben. ISBN: 9783784730196 (p.207 citing Report of Ludwig Reiter of 07.01.1946. IfZ, ZS/A4/7).

11. John Toland: *The Last 100 Days: The Tumultuous and Controversial Story of the Final Days of World War II in Europe*, 1966, reprint (2003) ISBN 0-44092621-1. (p.472-3)

12. Rupprecht Gerngross: *"Fasanenjagd" und wie die Münchner Freiheit ihren Namen bekam. Erinnerungen des Dr. Rupprecht Gerngross*. Augsburg: Heidrich, 1995. ISBN 3-930455-92-7. (p.99)

13. Veronika Diem: *Die Freiheitsaktion Bayern: ein Aufstand in der Endphase des NS-Regimes*, 2013. Kallmünz/Opf: Verlag Michael Lassleben. ISBN: 9783784730196 (p.407 citing *Abschliessender*

Tatsachenbericht der FAB (Concluding Report about the Activities of FAB) date unknown BayHSta, Abteilung IV, Handschriftensammlung 2347)

14. Veronika Diem: *Die Freiheitsaktion Bayern: ein Aufstand in der Endphase des NS-Regimes*, 2013. Kallmünz/Opf: Verlag Michael Lassleben. ISBN: 9783784730196 (p.261 citing transcript of the statement made by Hans Mayerhöfer 20.06.1947. StAM, Staatsanwaltschaften 18848/2).

15. Veronika Diem: *Die Freiheitsaktion Bayern Ein Aufstand im April 1945 und seine Folgen: Inauguraldissertation zur Erlangung des Doktorgrades der Philosophie and der Ludwig-Maximilians-Universität München.* 2011 (p.259 citing handwritten notes of Dr Alfred Harms (version 2), The memories of Franz Xaver Ritter von Epp date unknown but some time during the summer of 46. BayHStA Abteilung IV, Nachlass Epp 93)

16. Interview with Rupprecht Gerngross, Haus der Bayerischen Geschichte Museum, Regensburg, Germany. Verbatim record PR-Nr. 363/6 *Zeitzeugen zur Bayerischen Geschichte* recorded 24/25.4.1989 Munich. (p.12)

17. Helga Pfoertner. *Mit der Geschichte Leben: Mahnmale, Gedenkstätten, Erinnerungsorte für die Opfer des Nationalsozialismus in München 1933-45* Band 1, A bis H (p. 35) citing Heinrich Frese in Gerhard K. F. Stinglwagner (1991): Von Mönchen, Prinzen und Ministern (p.185)

CHAPTER TEN

1. Veronika Diem: *Die Freiheitsaktion Bayern: ein Aufstand in der Endphase des NS-Regimes*, 2013. Kallmünz/Opf: Verlag Michael Lassleben. ISBN: 9783784730196 (p.253 citing Beurteilungsnotiz for Officers 15.3.1945 BArch PERS 6/643)

2. Rupprecht Gerngross: *"Fasanenjagd" und wie die Münchner Freiheit ihren Namen bekam. Erinnerungen des Dr. Rupprecht Gerngross*. Augsburg: Heidrich, 1995. ISBN 3-930455-92-7. (p.132)

3. Veronika Diem: *Die Freiheitsaktion Bayern: ein Aufstand in der Endphase des NS-Regimes*, 2013. Kallmünz/Opf: Verlag Michael Lassleben. ISBN: 9783784730196 (p.258 citing transcript of the statement of Friedrich Tschelofiga of 03.07.1947. StAM, Staatsanwaltschaften 18848/2).

4. Veronika Diem: *Die Freiheitsaktion Bayern: ein Aufstand in der Endphase des NS-Regimes*, 2013. Kallmünz/Opf: Verlag Michael Lassleben. ISBN: 9783784730196 (pp.277-8 citing transcript of the statement of Dr Anton Ernstberger in the public sitting of Strafkammer 3 of Landgericht München I, actual trial of the criminal case against Alfred Salisco and two others of 24.11.1947. StAM, Staatsanwaltschaften18848/2).

5. Veronika Diem: *Die Freiheitsaktion Bayern Ein Aufstand im April 1945 und seine Folgen: Inauguraldissertation zur Erlangung des Doktorgrades der Philosophie and der Ludwig-Maximilians-Universität München*. 2011 (p.275 citing Percy Schramm: *Kriegstagebuch des Oberkommandos der Wehrmacht (Wehrmachtführungsstab)*. Band 4/2: 1940-45. January 1944-22 May 1945. Herrsching 1982.

(pp. 1448-1449)

6. Interview with Rupprecht Gerngross, Haus der Bayerischen Geschichte Museum, Regensburg, Germany. Verbatim record PR-Nr. 363/6 *Zeitzeugen zur Bayerischen Geschichte* recorded 24/25.4.1989 Munich. (p.4)

7. Veronika Diem: *Die Freiheitsaktion Bayern: ein Aufstand in der Endphase des NS-Regimes*, 2013. Kallmünz/Opf: Verlag Michael Lassleben. ISBN: 9783784730196 (p.246 citing the report of Josef Berger of 20.01.1946. IfZ, ZS/A4/6)

8. A copy of the leaflet dated 25.04.1945 is held in the Statdtarchiv in Munich.

9. Here and following: Veronika Diem: *Die Freiheitsaktion Bayern: ein Aufstand in der Endphase des NS-Regimes*, 2013. Kallmünz/Opf: Verlag Michael Lassleben. ISBN: 9783784730196 (*Eskalierte Folgeaktionen* pp.288-298) and Abendzeitung (Munich) of 28.04.2020 *Die Penzberger Mordnacht: Kriegsverbrechen in Oberbayern* by Karl Stankiewitz.

10. Josef Grimm LinkFang: de.linkfang.org/wiki/Josef-Grimm#cite_note-5 citing transcript of a letter to the *Gendarmerie* at Bruckmühl to the *Oberstaatsanwalt* at the Landgericht Traunstein of 29th April 1945. Staatsarchiv, Munich, Staatsanwaltschaften 31245/3 and photocopy of post-mortem certificate number 42 of April 1945 of the *Polizeibehörde* Aibling. Staatsarchiv, Munich. Staatsanwaltschaften 31245/3

11. altötting.de/unsere-stadt/stadtgeschichte/opfer-des-28-april-1945 and http://trend.infopartisan.net/trd1014/t071014.html

12. Veronika Diem: *Die Freiheitsaktion Bayern: ein Aufstand in der Endphase des NS-Regimes*, 2013. Kallmünz/Opf: Verlag Michael Lassleben. ISBN: 9783784730196 (p.270 citing a transcript of the statement of Alfred Salisco of 8.1.1947. StAM, Staatsanwaltschaften 18848/2)

13. Veronika Diem: *Die Freiheitsaktion Bayern Ein Aufstand im April 1945 und seine Folgen: Inauguraldissertation zur Erlangung des Doktorgrades der Philosophie and der Ludwig-Maximilians-Universität München.* 2011 (p.268 citing transcript of the statement of Alfred Salisco 8.1.1947. StAM, Staatsanwaltswchaften 18848/2.

14. Rupprecht Gerngross: *"Fasanenjagd" und wie die Münchner Freiheit ihren Namen bekam. Erinnerungen des Dr. Rupprecht Gerngross.* Augsburg: Heidrich, 1995. ISBN 3-930455-92-7. (pp.137-8)

15. Rupprecht Gerngross*: So was das damals 1945 mit der Freiheits-Aktion Bayern FAB. Erinnerungen an eine historische Begebenheit anläßlich der 25. Wiederkehr des Tages ders letzten Aufstandes gegen Hitler.* München 1970. Nachlass GG 15, BayHstA; Interview with Rupprecht Gerngross, Haus der Bayerischen Geschichte Museum, Regensburg, Germany. Verbatim record PR-Nr. 363/5 *Zeitzeugen zur Bayerischen Geschichte* recorded 24/25.4.1989 Munich. (p.12)

CHAPTER ELEVEN

1. Rebecca Boehling: *A Question of Priorities: Democratic Reforms and Economic Recovery in Postwar Germany.* Berghahn Books, U.S. 1996. ISBN: 978-1-57181-0359

(p.106 citing Michael Schattenhofer (ed.) *Chronik der Stadt München 1945-1948*. Munich 1980. (p.107 citing *New Yorker* magazine of May 13 1945)

2. Noel Newsome: *Giant at Bush House: At the heart of the radio war: The autobiography of Noel Newsome, Vol 1 1906-45*. The Real Press, UK. ISBN: 9781912119974. Chapter 28: *Excursion Behind the Enemy's Lines*. (pp402-3)

3. Here and following: Noel Newsome: *Giant at Bush House: At the heart of the radio war: The autobiography of Noel Newsome, Vol 1 1906-45*. The Real Press. UK. ISBN: 9781912119974. Chapter 28 *Excursion Behind the Enemy's Lines*.

4. Jeffrey S. Gaab: *Politics, Circumstance, Intelligence, Strategy: A Review of the U.S. Race to Munich and Capture of the "Alpine Redoubt "In World War Two*. Review of History and Political Science June 2016, Vol. 4, No. 1, pp. 1-11 ISSN: 2333-5726 (Online) Published by American Research Institute for Policy Development DOI: http://rhpsnet.com/journals/rhps/Vol_4_No_1_June_2016/1.pdf

5. Edith Raim: *"Kaufering 1-XI"*. 2009. In Geoffrey Megargee, (ed). *Early Camps, Youth Camps and Concentration Campsm and Subcamps under the SS-Business Administration Main Office (WVHA)*. Encyclopedia of Camps and Ghettos, 1933-45. Translated by Stephen Pallavicini. Bloomington: United States Holocaust Memorial Museum pp 488-490. ISBN 978-0-253-35328-3 (p.490)

6. Wikipedia citing Daniel Uziel: *Arming the Luftwaffe: The German Aviation Industry in World War II*.

Jefferson: (2011) McFarland. ISBN: 9780786488797

7. Here and following:
   http://scrapbookpages.com/DachauScrapbook/Dachau
   Liberation/

8. Margaret A. Salinger: *Dream Catcher: A
   Memoir*.Washington Square Press, New York. 2001.
   ISBN: 0671042823 (p.55)

9. Joseph E. Persico: *Piercing the Reich*. Viking Press. New
   York. 1979. ISBN: 0-670-55490-1 (p.306)

10. Jim Lankford: *The 14th Armored Division and the
    Liberation of Stalag VIIA, U.S. National Army Museum*
    (armyhistory.org/the-14th-armored-division-and-the-
    liberation-of-stalag-viia)

11. Haus der Bayerischen Geschichte Museum, Regensburg,
    Germany. Website page 12.3 Resistance during the Last
    Days:
    http://www.hdbg.de/dachau/pdfs/12/12_03/12_03_01.
    PDF

12. Nuremberg Trial Proceedings Volume 20: *One hundred
    and ninety-fifth day. Monday: 6 August 1946. Morning
    Session. Documents in Law, History and Diplomacy.*
    The Avalon Project. Lillian Goldman Law Library. Yale
    Law School. Evidence given by witness Karl Freiherr von
    Eberstein, Higher SS and Police Leader for military
    district VII in Munich. He was dismissed from the post
    by Giesler on April 20 1945 for "defeatism".

13. Süddeutsche Zeitung: *Von der SS erschossen.* 22.4.2015
    by Hans Holzhaider; Mark Felton in *Holocaust Heroes:
    Resistance to Hitler's Final Solution.* Pen and Sword
    books, Barnsley, UK. 2016. ISBN: 9781783400577)

14. Here and following: Bayerischer Rundfunk: *Thema*

*Kriegsende 1945. "Hauptstadt der Bewegung" ergibt
sich kampflos.* By Ernst Eisenbichler. 07.04.2015:
https://www.br.de/nachricht/inhalt/kriegsende-1945-
befreiung-muenchen-100.html

CHAPTER TWELVE

1. Here and following throughout chapter: Noel Newsome:
    *Giant at Bush House: At the heart of the radio war: The
    autobiography of Noel Newsome, Vol 1 1906-45*. The
    Real Press. UK. ISBN: 9781912119974. Chapter 28
    Excursion Behind the Enemy's Lines.

2. Rupprecht Gerngross: *"Fasanenjagd" und wie die
    Münchner Freiheit ihren Namen bekam. Erinnerungen
    des Dr. Rupprecht Gerngross*. Augsburg: Heidrich, 1995.
    ISBN 3-930455-92-7. (p.138).

3. David and Harry Lindauer: *A Soldier's Tale,* published
    by authorHouse ISBN 978-1-4969-1130-852395 citing
    military report M11 Team 449-G Report #28, 2 May
    1945.

4. Rebecca Boehling: *A Question of Priorities: Democratic
    Reforms and Economic Recovery in Postwar Germany*.
    Berghahn Books, U.S. 1996. ISBN: 978-1-57181-0359
    (p.106 citing Michael Schattenhofer (ed.) *Chronik der
    Stadt München 1945-1948* (Munich 1980. p.107)

5. Veronika Diem: *Die Freiheitsaktion Bayern: ein
    Aufstand in der Endphase des NS-Regimes*, 2013.
    Kallmünz/Opf: Verlag Michael Lassleben. ISBN:
    9783784730196 (pp.299-300 citing the Report of the
    Closing of the Investigative Proceedings against
    unknown people into the murder of Peace Negotiators in
    Bad Wiessee of 03.05.1945 dated 28.06.1971. StAM,

Staatsanwaltschaften 34735/4) and Report of Franz
Heiß to *Oberregierungsrat* Alois Braun 14.03.1946.
IfZ,ZS/A4/4; also citing Journal of U.S. 141st Infantry
regiment 03 and 04.05.1945. StAM,
Staatsanwaltschaften 34735/6 which confirms the
intention to bomb the town.

CHAPTER THIRTEEN

1. Interview with Rupprecht Gerngross, Haus der
   Bayerischen Geschichte Museum, Regensburg,
   Germany. Verbatim record PR-Nr. 363/6 *Zeitzeugen zur
   Bayerischen Geschichte* recorded 24/25.4.1989 Munich.
   (p.15)

2. Rupprecht Gerngross: *"Fasanenjagd" und wie die
   Münchner Freiheit ihren Namen bekam. Erinnerungen
   des Dr. Rupprecht Gerngross.* Augsburg: Heidrich, 1995.
   ISBN 3-930455-92-7. (p.147)

3. Rebecca Boehling: *Stunde Null: The End and the
   Beginning Fifty Years Ago.* Occasional Paper No.20.
   Edited by Geoffrey J. Giles. German Historical Institute.
   Washington, D.C. (p.125 citing Lutz Niethammer: *"Die
   Amerikanische Besatzungsmacht zwischen
   Verwaltungstradition und politischen Parteien in
   Bayern 1945,"*Vierteljahrshefte für Zeitgeschichte 15.
   1967 (p. 164)

4. Rupprecht Gerngross: *"Fasanenjagd" und wie die
   Münchner Freiheit ihren Namen bekam. Erinnerungen
   des Dr. Rupprecht Gerngross.* Augsburg: Heidrich, 1995.
   ISBN 3-930455-92-7. (p.138)

5. Interview with Rupprecht Gerngross, Haus der
   Bayerischen Geschichte Museum, Regensburg,

Germany. Verbatim record PR-Nr. 363/6 *Zeitzeugen zur Bayerischen Geschichte* recorded 24/25.4.1989 Munich. (p.10)

6. Here and following: Rupprecht Gerngross: *"Fasanenjagd" und wie die Münchner Freiheit ihren Namen bekam. Erinnerungen des Dr. Rupprecht Gerngross.* Augsburg: Heidrich, 1995. ISBN 3-930455-92-7. (p.139ff)

7. Rupprecht Gerngross: *"Fasanenjagd" und wie die Münchner Freiheit ihren Namen bekam. Erinnerungen des Dr. Rupprecht Gerngross.* Augsburg: Heidrich, 1995. ISBN 3-930455-92-7. (p.139)

8. Bayerische Landeszeitung published 01.06.1945, Number 2.

9. *Süddeutsche Zeitung* published 30.04.1946

10. *Süddeutsche Zeitung* published 03.09.1946

11. Rupprecht Gerngross: *"Fasanenjagd" und wie die Münchner Freiheit ihren Namen bekam. Erinnerungen des Dr. Rupprecht Gerngross.* Augsburg: Heidrich, 1995. ISBN 3-930455-92-7. (p.106)

12. Interview with Rupprecht Gerngross, Haus der Bayerischen Geschichte Museum, Regensburg, Germany. Verbatim record PR-Nr. 363/4 *Zeitzeugen zur Bayerischen Geschichte* recorded 24/25.4.1989 Munich. (pp. 16-17)

13. Karl Wieninger: *In München erlebte Geschichte,* Strumberger, München, 1985. ISBN: 9783921193211. (p.100)

14. Rupprecht Gerngross: *"Fasanenjagd" und wie die Münchner Freiheit ihren Namen bekam. Erinnerungen*

des Dr. Rupprecht Gerngross. Augsburg: Heidrich, 1995. ISBN 3-930455-92-7. (pp.147-8)

15. Rupprecht Gerngross: *"Fasanenjagd" und wie die Münchner Freiheit ihren Namen bekam. Erinnerungen des Dr. Rupprecht Gerngross.* Augsburg: Heidrich, 1995. ISBN 3-930455-92-7. (p.115)

16. Veronika Diem: *Die Freiheitsaktion Bayern Ein Aufstand im April 1945 und seine Folgen: Inauguraldissertation zur Erlangung des Doktorgrades der Philosophie and der Ludwig-Maximilians-Universität München.* 2011 (pp.253 citing, as an example, the transcript of the statement of Leonhard Würmseer of 16.07.1947. StAM, Staatsanwaltschaften 18848/2).

17. Veronika Diem: *Die Freiheitsaktion Bayern: ein Aufstand in der Endphase des NS-Regimes,* 2013. Kallmünz/Opf: Verlag Michael Lassleben. ISBN: 9783784730196 (p.260 citing judgement of the third Strafkammer of the Munich District Court 1 (Landgericht) against Alfred Salisco and others of 24.11.1947 StAM Staatsanwaltschaften 18848/2)

18. Veronika Diem: *Die Freiheitsaktion Bayern Ein Aufstand im April 1945 und seine Folgen: Inauguraldissertation zur Erlangung des Doktorgrades der Philosophie and der Ludwig-Maximilians-Universität München.* 2011 (p.279 citing transcript of the public sitting of Crimimal Court 3 of the *Landgericht,* Munich I. Trial of the criminal case against Alfred Salisco and two others of 24.11.1947. StAM, Staatsanwaltschaften 18848/2).

19. Veronika Diem: *Die Freiheitsaktion Bayern Ein Aufstand im April 1945 und seine Folgen:*

Inauguraldissertation zur Erlangung des Doktorgrades
der Philosophie and der Ludwig-Maximilians-
Universität München. 2011 (p.279 citing the judgement
of the third *Strafkammer* of the Munich District Court 1
against Rudolf Hübner of 25.11.1948 StAM,
Staatsanwaltschaften 19045/1).

20. Veronika Diem: *Die Freiheitsaktion Bayern Ein
Aufstand im April 1945 und seine Folgen:
Inauguraldissertation zur Erlangung des Doktorgrades
der Philosophie and der Ludwig-Maximilians-
Universität München.* 2011 (p.279 citing a transcript of
the statement of Alfons Berberich in the main hearing of
the first Strafkammer of Munich district court 1 against
Karl Noack for aiding murder of 14.5.46. StAM, GStAnw
366).

21. Interview with Rupprecht Gerngross, Haus der
Bayerischen Geschichte Museum, Regensburg,
Germany. Verbatim record PR-Nr. 363/6 *Zeitzeugen zur
Bayerischen Geschichte* recorded 24/25.4.1989 Munich.
(p.12)

22. Rupprecht Gerngross: *"Fasanenjagd" und wie die
Münchner Freiheit ihren Namen bekam. Erinnerungen
des Dr. Rupprecht Gerngross.* Augsburg: Heidrich, 1995.
ISBN 3-930455-92-7. (p.135 citing court files of
Landesgericht München I: Judgement of 24.11.1947, Az:
1a JS 1644/46-47)

23. Karl Wieninger: *In München erlebte Geschichte,*
Strumberger, München, 1985. ISBN: 9783921193211.
(p.97)

24. Veronika Diem: *Die Freiheitsaktion Bayern: ein
Aufstand in der Endphase des NS-Regimes,* 2013.
Kallmünz/Opf: Verlag Michael Lassleben. ISBN:

9783784730196 (p.276 citing a transcript of the statement of Jakob Vogl of 9.10.1945 and 02.07.1948 from the public sitting of the third *Strafkammer* of Munich District Court I of 2.07.1948. StAM, Staatsanwaltschaften 18849/1)

25. Thomas Martin: *Aspekte der politischen Biographie eines lokalen NS-Funktionärs, Der Fall Christian Weber* in Zeitschrift für Bayerische Landesgeschichte. Bayerische Staatsbibliothek. ZBLG 57 1994 (p. 479). https://periodika.digitale-sammlungen.de//zblg/seite/zblg57_0499

26. Veronika Diem: *Die Freiheitsaktion Bayern: ein Aufstand in der Endphase des NS-Regimes*, 2013. Kallmünz/Opf: Verlag Michael Lassleben. ISBN: 9783784730196 (p.287 citing the registered entry of the *Kriminalinspektion 1/1* of 6.11.1959 and the concluding report of 03.12.1959. StAM, Staatsanwaltschaften 21319).

27. Veronika Diem: *Die Freiheitsaktion Bayern Ein Aufstand im April 1945 und seine Folgen: Inauguraldissertation zur Erlangung des Doktorgrades der Philosophie and der Ludwig-Maximilians-Universität München*. 2011 (pp.289-90 citing a letter from Anton Gründl of 03.08.1987 published verbatim in: Herbert Dandl: *"Fort mit dem Verbrecher!". Spuren politischen Widerstands gegen das NS-Regime in Giesing*. In: Thomas Guttman (editor): *Unter den Dächern von Giesing. Politik und Alltag 1918-1945. Beiträge zur Geschichte Giesings und Harlachings von der Revolution bis zum Ende des Zweiten Weltkriegs*. Munich 1993. (pp.111-128)

28. Veronika Diem: *Die Freiheitsaktion Bayern Ein*

Aufstand im April 1945 und seine Folgen: Inauguraldissertation zur Erlangung des Doktorgrades der Philosophie and der Ludwig-Maximilians-Universität München. 2011 (p.352 citing Turicum to Information Control Division *"Spannungen in der FAB"* 26.04.1946. IfZ, MA 1479/13).

29. Veronika Diem: *Die Freiheitsaktion Bayern Ein Aufstand im April 1945 und seine Folgen: Inauguraldissertation zur Erlangung des Doktorgrades der Philosophie and der Ludwig-Maximilians-Universität München.* 2011 (p.355 citing a letter from archive director Dr Schattenhöfer, Stadtarchiv, München to the Direktorium, Verwaltungsamt of 16.08.1965 and of 10.12.1965. StadtA München, Direktorium Abgabe 3/18, Nr. 30).

30. Veronika Diem: *Die Freiheitsaktion Bayern Ein Aufstand im April 1945 und seine Folgen: Inauguraldissertation zur Erlangung des Doktorgrades der Philosophie and der Ludwig-Maximilians-Universität München.* 2011 (p.355 citing entry on 13.05.1975 in the documents of the reords department of Landeshauptstadt Munich).

31. Die Zeit newspaper 25.04.1975

32. Stern magazine17.04.1975

33. Veronika Diem: *Die Freiheitsaktion Bayern Ein Aufstand im April 1945 und seine Folgen: Inauguraldissertation zur Erlangung des Doktorgrades der Philosophie and der Ludwig-Maximilians-Universität München.* 2011 (pp.375-6 citing Süddeutsche Zeitung of 29.04.1981).

34. Veronika Diem: *Die Freiheitsaktion Bayern Ein*

Aufstand im April 1945 und seine Folgen: Inauguraldissertation zur Erlangung des Doktorgrades der Philosophie and der Ludwig-Maximilians-Universität München. 2011 (p.359 citing a letter from Gerngross to Lutz Kretlau and Herr Maier of 05.09.1989. Nachlass Gerngross 51. BayHStA).

35. Veronika Diem: *Die Freiheitsaktion Bayern Ein Aufstand im April 1945 und seine Folgen: Inauguraldissertation zur Erlangung des Doktorgrades der Philosophie and der Ludwig-Maximilians-Universität München.* 2011 (p.372 citing Helga Pfoertner. *Mit der Geschichte Leben: Mahnmale, Gedenkstätten, Erinnerungsorte für die Opfer des Nationalsozialismus in München 1933-45* Band 1, A bis H (p. 35-38, 68-70 and 127-8 and Bäumler Klaus: NS-Dokumentationszentrum in Königsplatz. Zum Gedenktag für die Opfer des Nationalsozialismus 2002. Munich 2002. p.4).

36. Süddeutsche Zeitung of 30.04/01.05.1984 and Münchner Merkur of 14.05.1984

CHAPTER FOURTEEN

1. Here and following: Karl Wieninger: *In München erlebte Geschichte,* Strumberger, München, 1985. ISBN: 9783921193211. (p.97); Howard Becker: *The Nature and Consequences of Black Propaganda.* In: American Sociological Review Volume 14 Number 2 (1949) Pp.221-235 (p.232-3)

2. Transcript of *Bayerischer Rundfunk* broadcast of Bernhard Ücker of Saturday 16th November 1968.22.05-22.45 Uhr. II Programm. Nachlass Gerngross 15 II Materialsammlung. BayHstA

3. Howard Becker; *The Nature and Consequences of Black Propaganda* in: American Sociological Review.Vol. 14, No.2 (April 1949). American Sociological Association. (pp.221-235: p.233)

4. Interview with Rupprecht Gerngross, Haus der Bayerischen Geschichte Museum, Regensburg, Germany. Verbatim record PR-Nr. 363/6 *Zeitzeugen zur Bayerischen Geschichte* recorded 24/25.4.1989 Munich. (p.28)

5. Veronika Diem: *Die Freiheitsaktion Bayern Ein Aufstand im April 1945 und seine Folgen: Inauguraldissertation zur Erlangung des Doktorgrades der Philosophie and der Ludwig-Maximilians-Universität München.* 2011 (p.393 citing Joachim Brückner: *Kreigsende in Bayern 1945. Der Wehrkreis VII und die Kämpfe zwischen Donau und Alpen* (Einzelschriften zur militärischen Geschichte des Zweiten Weltkrieges 30). Freiburg 1987. (p.189, 192 and 195)

6. Ian Kershaw: *The End: Hitler's Germany 1944-45.* Allen Lane, London 2011. ISBN: 9780713997163. (p.343)

7. Veronika Diem: *Die Freiheitsaktion Bayern Ein Aufstand im April 1945 und seine Folgen: Inauguraldissertation zur Erlangung des Doktorgrades der Philosophie and der Ludwig-Maximilians-Universität München.* 2011 (p.301)

8. Veronika Diem: *Die Freiheitsaktion Bayern: ein Aufstand in der Endphase des NS-Regimes*, 2013. Kallmünz/Opf: Verlag Michael Lassleben. ISBN: 9783784730196 (p.160)

9. Veronika Diem: *Die Freiheitsaktion Bayern Ein*

Aufstand im April 1945 und seine Folgen: Inauguraldissertation zur Erlangung des Doktorgrades der Philosophie and der Ludwig-Maximilians-Universität München. 2011 (p.242)

10. Veronika Diem: *Die Freiheitsaktion Bayern Ein Aufstand im April 1945 und seine Folgen: Inauguraldissertation zur Erlangung des Doktorgrades der Philosophie and der Ludwig-Maximilians-Universität München.* 2011 (p.312)

11. Veronika Diem: *Die Freiheitsaktion Bayern: ein Aufstand in der Endphase des NS-Regimes*, 2013. Kallmünz/Opf: Verlag Michael Lassleben. ISBN: 9783784730196 (pp.361) and Veronika Diem: *Die Freiheitsaktion Bayern Ein Aufstand im April 1945 und seine Folgen: Inauguraldissertation zur Erlangung des Doktorgrades der Philosophie and der Ludwig-Maximilians-Universität München.* 2011 (p.360, p.309 and p.395)

12. Interview with Rupprecht Gerngross, Haus der Bayerischen Geschichte Museum, Regensburg, Germany. Verbatim record PR-Nr. 363/6 *Zeitzeugen zur Bayerischen Geschichte* recorded 24/25.4.1989 Munich. (p.3)

13. Interview with Rupprecht Gerngross, Haus der Bayerischen Geschichte Museum, Regensburg, Germany. Verbatim record PR-Nr. 363/6 *Zeitzeugen zur Bayerischen Geschichte* recorded 24/25.4.1989 Munich. (p.4)

14. Report by Dachau police detective in Nachlass *Materialsammlung II Buchstabe 3-D*, Nachlass Gerngross 15, BayHStA.

15. Veronika Diem: *Die Freiheitsaktion Bayern Ein Aufstand im April 1945 und seine Folgen: Inauguraldissertation zur Erlangung des Doktorgrades der Philosophie and der Ludwig-Maximilians-Universität München.* 2011 (p.160 citing Wilhelm Arendts, a friend of Halder's, from a conversation 04.09.1943. Spruchkammerverfahren 1948. Transcript of 28.03.1948. StAM, Spruchkammerakten K 34 Arendts, Wilhelm and p.162 citing an interview with Dr Otto Leibrecht in Munich 19.06.1945 in a Report on Black Operations in Today's Germany by Howard Becker, Edmund Reiss and Rudolf Weiss 13.07.1945. NARA 226/92/587/41).

16. Rupprecht Gerngross: *"Fasanenjagd" und wie die Münchner Freiheit ihren Namen bekam. Erinnerungen des Dr. Rupprecht Gerngross.* Augsburg: Heidrich, 1995. ISBN 3-930455-92-7. (p.113)

17. Letter from Czech concentration camp survivor Ferdinand Zilinsky to a newspaper in 1957 from his native Czechoslovakia in.Rupprecht Gerngross: *"So war das damals 1945 mit der Freiheitsaktion Bayern. Erinnerungen an eine historische Begebenheit anläßlich der Wiederkehr des Tages des letzten Aufstandes gegen Hitler.* Herausgegeben im Eigenverlag. München 1970. Nachlass Gerngross 21, BayHStA

18. Interview with Rupprecht Gerngross, Haus der Bayerischen Geschichte Museum, Regensburg, Germany. Verbatim record PR-Nr. 363/4 *Zeitzeugen zur Bayerischen Geschichte* recorded 24/25.4.1989 Munich. (p.19)

19. Executive Intelligence Review, Volume 21, Number 29. Christophe Lavehrne: *Lessons of Anti-Nazi Resistance*

Invoked at Lyon Conference. July 22nd 1994.
https://larouchepub.com/eiw/public/1994/eirv21n29-19940722/index.html

20. *Wittenstein Lecture Series*, 2010, Germanic and Slavic
Studies, University of California, Santa Barbara
gss.ucsb.edu/news/conferences/wittenstein *and 'The
White Rose: Student Resistance in Germany During
WWII* by John Grinder September 1, 2001 Nuclear Age
Peace Foundation. https://wagingpeace.org.the-white-rose-student-resistance-in-Germany-during-wwii

21. Bayerischer Rundfunk: *Felix Heidenberger "im
Gespräch" mit Gabi Toepsch* Sendung von 08.05.2008
20.15 Uhr: BR-online.

22. Veronika Diem: *Die Freiheitsaktion Bayern Ein
Aufstand im April 1945 und seine Folgen:
Inauguraldissertation zur Erlangung des Doktorgrades
der Philosophie and der Ludwig-Maximilians-
Universität München.* 2011 (p.393)

23. Veronika Diem: *Die Freiheitsaktion Bayern Ein
Aufstand im April 1945 und seine Folgen:
Inauguraldissertation zur Erlangung des Doktorgrades
der Philosophie and der Ludwig-Maximilians-
Universität München.* 2011 (p.351 citing Erich Kästner:
Notabene 45. Ein Tagebuch. Berlin 1961. p.106)

24. Rupprecht Gerngross: *"Fasanenjagd" und wie die
Münchner Freiheit ihren Namen bekam. Erinnerungen
des Dr. Rupprecht Gerngross.* Augsburg: Heidrich, 1995.
ISBN 3-930455-92-7. (p.115 and p.32)

25. Rupprecht Gerngross: *"Fasanenjagd" und wie die
Münchner Freiheit ihren Namen bekam. Erinnerungen
des Dr. Rupprecht Gerngross.* Augsburg: Heidrich, 1995.

ISBN 3-930455-92-7. (p.32 and Foreword p.9)

26. Rupprecht Gerngross: *"Fasanenjagd" und wie die Münchner Freiheit ihren Namen bekam. Erinnerungen des Dr. Rupprecht Gerngross.* Augsburg: Heidrich, 1995. ISBN 3-930455-92-7. (p.116)

27. Rupprecht Gerngross: *"Fasanenjagd" und wie die Münchner Freiheit ihren Namen bekam. Erinnerungen des Dr. Rupprecht Gerngross.* Augsburg: Heidrich, 1995. ISBN 3-930455-92-7. (p.146)

28. Rupprecht Gerngross: *"Fasanenjagd" und wie die Münchner Freiheit ihren Namen bekam. Erinnerungen des Dr. Rupprecht Gerngross.* Augsburg: Heidrich, 1995. ISBN 3-930455-92-7. *Foreword* (p.9)

29. Rupprecht Gerngross: *"Fasanenjagd" und wie die Münchner Freiheit ihren Namen bekam. Erinnerungen des Dr. Rupprecht Gerngross.* Augsburg: Heidrich, 1995. ISBN 3-930455-92-7. (p.93)

30. Rupprecht Gerngross: *"Fasanenjagd" und wie die Münchner Freiheit ihren Namen bekam. Erinnerungen des Dr. Rupprecht Gerngross.* Augsburg: Heidrich, 1995. ISBN 3-930455-92-7. (p.10)

The Real Press

If you enjoyed this book, take a look at the other books we have on our list at www.therealpress.co.uk